Protestantism the Modern Tower of Babel

Protestantism the Modern Tower of Babel

Robert F. Kopfer

Copyright © 2006 Robert F. Kopfer
All rights reserved.

ISBN : 1-4196-4938-8

To order additional copies, please contact us.
BookSurge, LLC
www.booksurge.com
1-866-308-6235
orders@booksurge.com

Protestantism the Modern Tower of Babel

Prologue	Seed is planted	xi
Chapter 1	The beginning	1
Chapter 2	The modern Tower of Babel	5
Chapter 3	The early days	9
Chapter 4	Faith and Deeds	17
Chapter 5	Homosexuality	21
Chapter 6	Marionalogy	29
Chapter 7	Stigmata	41
Chapter 8	The Protestant Bible	47
Chapter 9	One Fold and One shepherd	67
Chapter 10	Past wrongs of the Catholic Church and the Reformation	73
Chapter 11	Contradictions of the Protestant Faiths	83
Chapter 12	Divide and Conquer Dilute and Destroy	93
Chapter 13	Sins of the Clerics	103
Chapter 14	Theology of the Founders of the Reformation	111
Chapter 15	Sins of the Founders of the Reformation	125
Chapter 16	Martin Luther Saint or Sinner Hero or Rogue	141
Chapter 17	Sola Scriptura	153
Chapter 18	Sola Fide	169
Chapter 19	Survey results and commentary	177
Epilogue		195

An Implication of the Divergence of Christian Theology as a Result of the Calvin / Melanchthon Impasse

John Calvin warned Phillip Melanchthon, Luther's successor, that unless there was unity among the various factions in the Reformation, that the understanding of Scripture would be diluted. As a result he predicted that many "false prophets" would arise and lead many Souls away from the True Teaching of Jesus Christ. See if you concur.

Prologue

A Seed Is Planted

For as long as I can remember, whenever I had a discussion with someone regarding religion, the first comments that they made in defending their "faith" or the reason why they left the Catholic Church was , "the trouble with Catholics" and they would go on from there.

Regarding my Faith, I guess I can be classified both as a *"Cradle Catholic"* and as a *"Born Again Christian"*. As a Cradle Catholic I was born into my Faith. While my parents were not "Sunday go ta Meetin" Catholics, they were very strong in their Catholic beliefs. As part of the Marriage vows, *they* promised then (as I believe it still is today) to raise their Children in the Catholic Faith. They *honored* those vows.

When I graduated from grammar school , my father told me that he had fulfilled his obligation, and now the choice was mine to make. For several years, while I did not deny the Church, I did not participate in its functions and just drifted, until one night I was *"visited"* in a dream, by two Angels, who **"planted the Seed of Faith,"** in me and helped to set me on my Path to Christ.

As a "Born again Christian", it has not been an easy path. There were times when I questioned my Path and the "Weeds" of Doubt threatened to engulf my Faith. But the more I looked into the Teachings, the more I am convinced that I am on the right Path.

Time and again, when I discussed religion with someone who was of another religious persuasion, or had given up on their Catholic Faith, their standard reply started with "the trouble with the Catholic Church", and then they would go on from there. When I asked of them what they found in their new church (faith) they invariable came up with one of the following *excuses.*

The Trouble with the Catholic Church, etc, etc, etc.
- I don't like the priest
- I don't like the people
- The Masses are too long
- I don't like kneeling
- The Masses are too crowded
- They have lousy music
- The choir is bad
- The priest can't give a good sermon
- The other church is more entertaining
- The people are friendlier
- I don't like someone telling me what a "sin" is
- **"They"** were there when **I needed help**
- The sex scandals by the priests

Most people I talked to chose their new faith because of anti-catholic feelings or because the 'new church" allowed them to choose what they wanted to believe in, or they adopted the Faith of their spouse.

There was one individual, I met, and who had embraced the Catholic Faith. I asked what brought him to accept Catholicism. He told me, that while in World War II, he witnessed a priest, risking his life to administer the "Last Rites" to a dying G I. My response to him was that that really is not a good reason to join a Faith, as in ALL Faiths there are Hero's and Charlatans. It should be for the **One True Teaching of Jesus**.

Another incident I came across, was a young woman, brought up in the Catholic Faith, who joined a Nondenominational Faith. When I asked her why this faith, her reply was that it really does not matter which "Christian" church you attend, they are all the same. My reply was that she is either naive or lying.

Her pastor was supposed to "enlighten" me regarding "his" church. Several attempts were made to have this meeting of minds, but to no avail. Finally, in reply to an email, I was told "if I am looking for the One True Church of Jesus. I should pray to the Holy Ghost for guidance."

Finally, after much persistence on my part, the young woman blurted out, that she joined this new faith because the Catholics are all hypocrites. What a terrible blow this must have been to her family. Her mother was a stay at home mother, who devoted her life to her children. She volunteered at school to help out. She volunteered to drive mentally challenged women to their doctor's appointments. Her Godfather left school after 8th grade to go to work to help support the family. Dear friends of the family were also involved in many act of charity. These entire individuals were staunch Catholics. Yet, did she not look upon them as hypocrites?

Not one person gave me a reason, such as:

"I found the ONE TRUE TEACHINGS OF Jesus Christ"

I

The beginning

From the 16th century on, those who oppose the Catholic Church, but say they believe in Jesus Christ have been called "Protestants", but in reality are they not *Cafeteria Christians*? When we go to the cafeteria, we pick and choose what we want. So it is with those who choose a path contrary to the Catholic Teachings. In reality do not Protestants pick and choose which of the Teachings of Our Lord they want to accept?

In my search for the "Truth" I have found that there are well over 25,000 Churches that profess to expound the Teachings of Jesus Christ. Each of the 25,000 has a somewhat different concept of His Teachings. They ALL can't be right. Which one of them is right in their "teachings?

To my personal thinking, the Reformation was ONE of the Greatest Disasters to befall Christianity. What did it accomplish? The impediment that Martin Luther railed against has a very long time ago been rectified. Even as Martin Luther created a Schism with the Catholic Church, some of his followers have created other schisms within the Lutheran Faith and in the process are responsible for well over *twenty five thousand* or more "Christian" sects.

As the Church resolved the impediment of Copernicus and the Spanish Inquisition, so it resolved the complaint of Martin Luther. While the Spanish Inquisition was a painful part of Christian history, one must consider the times. Islam was threatening Europe on the East by attacking through the Balkans and also occupied Northern Africa, plus half of the Iberian Peninsula.

With Islam, "infidels" accepted Islam or were either executed or put into slavery. The usual mode of punishment was being sent to the galleys for the men. This was a "living" death. The women were sold into slavery to serve as sex objects. Those who were unable to be an asset or could not be ransomed were executed by most barbarbic means.

While Martin Luther may have been right in his complaint, he (to me) was wrong in his actions. In today's vernacular, it would be tantamount to *"throwing out the baby with the bath water"*. What did it accomplish? It helped to create thousands of "Christian" sects, each Faith going in a *different* direction.

Henry VIII of England followed Martin Luther's lead in challenging the authority of the Pope. When Henry was not granted a divorce or an annulment, Henry set himself up as the head of the Church of England. Ironically, the Church of England today frowns upon divorce. One of the very, very, few Protestant Faiths that do.

Henry over came this obstacle in the future by charging his later wives with treason or adultery and then had them executed. No need for a divorce then.

Both of the original Protestant sects were born in blood. In the case of Martin Luther, he advised the German Nobility to refrain from sending aid to Hungary which was being threatened by Suleiman. Luther had declared that Suleiman was the "Wrath of God" sent to punish the Catholics for their "sins". As a consequence, the entire Hungarian army and Nobility were slaughtered in the battle of Mohacs on August 29th, 1526. With the Hungarian army decimated the invasion route to Vienna and Central Europe was opened. Luther then saw the error of his edict and then published his **De Bello Trucia,** acknowledging that the Turks were the *"Enemy of God"*. The Germans rallied to the defense of Vienna and defeated Suleiman, ending, for the time being the Islamic invasion of Central Europe.

Let us for a moment imagine that the Founding Fathers of the Reformation were composing a Symphony. A Symphony of the Four Gospels. As the four Gospels had Mark Mathew Luke and John, the Founding Fathers would consist of Luther, Calvin Zwingali and Henry VIII. These players, along with several other miner participants would endeavor to compose and conduct the Great Masterpiece.

The Masterpiece:
"Rhapsody in Sola Scriptura"
By
Martin Luther, in collaboration with
John Calvin, Huldreich Zwingali, and Henry Tudor
Variations of Theme
By
John Wesley, Richard Allen, Francis Asbury, Konrad Gribel, John Smyth, Mary Baker Eddy, C.P Jones, Joseph Smith, John Cotton, Charles Taze Russell, Jim Jones et al, etc, etc, etc.

Imagine, if you will, Martin Luther leading the violin section. However as the ELCA, LCMS, and the WELS while looking to Luther, each has their own variation of the Theme, in both Key and Tempo.

With John Calvin leading the Woodwinds, we have at clarinet the Arianists. At Oboe we have the Huguenots, along with the Bassoons we have the Puritans, join with the Presbyterians at Flute. Again we have each of these followers of Calvin, doing their own interpretation. Playing in a different Key and Tempo, and half an octave off the Score.

At piano we have dual pianos, Anglican and Episcopalian. They should be following the lead of (Arch bishop) Rowan Williams. However he does seem to be exasperated as no one is following his lead. It may very well be that he has no idea as to which way to go. No one is following his lead.

With Zwingali leading the percussions, we have the SBC, ABC, NBC, and the NBCA all having a vastly different interpretation of the Score, and each playing in their own Tempo and Key.

Finally we come to the Brass. Bugles Trumpets, Horns, Trombones, and Saxophones. These players are classified as Nondenominational. John Smyth (Seventh Day Adventists) , with David Koresh deviating from John's lead. Then there is Mary Baker Eddy (Christian Science) having her own interpretation of how the Score should be presented. Follow this with C P Jones (Church of God in Christ), and Charles Taze Russell (Jehovah's Witnesses , and also Jim Jones (People's Temple).

Here we have an Orchestra, ostensibly performing from the **same** Score, but EACH one interpreting the Score (Bible) as they see fit. You can imagine what sound would have come from this assembly of musicians (Protestant Ministers). Twenty five thousand (25,000) musicians (ministers) each "touting" his/hers own interpretation of the Rhapsody (Scripture).

The Sound that would come from that Symphony Orchestra could best be described as *Cacophonous*. So here we have a new name for the "Rhapsody in Sola Scriptura". I would rename it:

Protestantism
The modern Tower of Babel

2

A Survey on the various Protestant Faiths

I would suggest, that before attempting to read and understand my findings, that you read and try to answer the question in the survey, then, at the end see how the Teachings you receive from your Church, compares with that of the other Protestant Faiths.

1. Denomination of your Church
2. Source of the ordination of your Pastor
3. Is your Denomination the "ONE TRUE TEACHING OF JESUS CHRIST
4. Which denomination is the One True Church of Jesus Christ
5. Is Baptism a Sacrament
6. Was Calvin justified in the sentence imposed on Servetus
7. Which Lutheran denomination follows the Original Teachings of Luther
8. Is sex outside of marriage fornication
9. Is Timothy St Paul's brother
10. Was Jesus born of a Virgin
11. Was Calvin correct in his prediction to Melanchthon
12. Is Communion a Sacrament
13. Is Tradition a basis in fact for teaching Christian Theology
14. Is Phillip St Peter's brother

15. Is sex between men an acceptable Christian life style
16. Do you believe in Purgatory, a condition before Heaven
17. Is the Rite of Marriage a Sacrament
18. Do you believe that Jesus had siblings through Mary
19. Is dancing a Sin
20. Has any member of your denomination experienced the Stigmata
21. Has any member of you Denomination been "visited" by a Saint
22. Is partaking of alcohol a sin
23. In Communion , is the Body and Blood of Christ present
24. Should an infant be Baptized
25. Should the Ordination of a Minister / Priest be a Sacrament
26. Do you believe that St Peter was in Rome
27. In your Denomination, what is the source of authority for interpretation of Scripture
28. Is Sola Scriptura the basis of your Faith
29. Should your Denomination "Bless" a union between homosexuals
30. Do you pray to Saint to intercede for you
31. Is the game of "chance " a sin
32. Is Oral or Anal sex an acceptable Christian life style
33. Is Abortion an acceptable Christian practice
34. At what point does life begin
35. Is Purgatory exclusively a Catholic belief
36. When were the Four Gospels declared HOLY SCRIPTURE and by what body
37. Should a marriage between brother and sister be acceptable
38. Is prostitution an acceptable Christian life style
39. Does a Priest / Minister have authority to forgive Sins

40. Should a man be allowed to have two or more wives
41. Should a marriage between uncle and niece / aunt and nephew be an acceptable Christian Life style
42. Do you believe in Hell
43. Do you believe in Predestination
44. Do you believe that Faith Alone (Sola Fide) will secure Salvation
45. Do you believe that "Good Works" alone will secure Salvation
46. Do you believe that Islam is a threat to Christianity
47. Do you believe that Islam and Christianity can coexist
48. Do you believe that Martin Luther was justified in his praise of Suleiman
49. Was Martin Luther correct in his belief that "any plowman can interpret Scripture"
50. Is the Anglican and Lutheran Faiths wrong in continuing dialogue concerning reunification with Rome

3

The early days

In the 1950's and 60's there was a group of evangelists that would come to your door on a Saturday or Sunday "claiming to preach the Bible", and touting the "Watch Tower" magazine. It did not take me long to see that they were in reality preaching Anti-Catholicism. One man in particular, after a long dissertation against the Catholic Church, said to me, quoting Chapter and Verse, without opening his bible, "you Catholics are so smug, in that you think yours is the only Church. But Scripture says;
  <u>and other Sheep I have that are not of this Fold</u>.
  What do you have to say to that?"
  I replied that "I believed that there is another sentence to that passage. Please open your bible and read it to me". When he opened his bible and looked up the passage, he closed his book, turned and walked away. Never to return.
  "There Shall be <u>One Fold</u> and <u>One Shepherd</u>"

Very many Protestants do believe that they are following the True Path, and living Christ's Teachings. However, believing you are right does not necessarily make it true. To me, it is that believing 2 +3 = 6. What many Protestant leaders do, is to take the + sign and tilt it so it appears as an x. Then the teaching becomes 2 x 3 = 6. By changing the equation, they have (to them) justified their answer. But is it the True Teaching of Jesus Christ?

To those who believe they are on the Right Path, I would cite an incident that occurred many years ago, that proved that believing you are Right does not make it True.

I would cite an incident that happened just before the start of World War I. A diplomat was arriving from the Balkans on an ocean liner. He was to partake in a peace conference in New York city. The diplomat held a press conference onboard the liner. An assassin approached and fired a shot that struck the diplomat in the upper arm. While the newsmen fought to subdue the assassin, a Boy Scout ran to the fallen diplomat, and removing his own belt, tied a tourniquet around the diplomat's arm. The Scout *believed* he was doing the right procedure.

It appeared that the young man was doing the "right" thing, in attempting to save the Diplomat's life, but the man died from loss of blood. The tourniquet was applied *below* the wound instead of *above* it. The technique of applying a tourniquet was followed, except for one small detail. That one detail made the procedure wrong. Missing that one "minor" detail resulted in death.

Protestants believe that they are right in their Beliefs. But did not Our Lord say, "not all who say, Lord, Lord, will be Saved, but only those who do the
Will of My Father."

Following is a list of some of the Teaching found in Scripture. In each one, different Protestant Sects, teach vastly different interpretation.
- The Primacy of Peter
- The Sanctity of Marriage
- Forgiveness of Sins
- Divorce
- Adultery
- Fornication
- Stigmata
- Homosexuality
- Pedophilia
- Incest

- Angels
- Saints
- Heaven
- Hell
- Virginity of Mary, the Mother of Jesus
- Interpretation of Scripture
- Abortion
- Faith and Good Works
- Miracles
- Holy Spirit

THE PRIMACY OF PETER
Thou art Peter, and upon This Rock I will Build My Church
And the Gates of Hell <u>Shall Not Prevail Against It</u>

In my early youth, I marveled at how Protestants could recite Chapter and Verse from Scripture. After a while I noted that for the most part they were referring to the Old Testament. Seldom did they quote New Testament Scripture. In listening to Protestant clergy and reading their Bible, I heard and read several different explanations as to their rejection of the Primacy of Peter.

One Book had as a footnote, regarding Peter, stating that "it is only mentioned once in Scripture, so therefore it can't be very relevant." I do take umbrage to that philosophy. First of all there are several references regarding Peter's recognition of Jesus as the "Christ" as coming from **Devine Inspiration**. But also, if we accept that if a passage appears only once in Scripture, that it could be dismissed as being irrelevant. If that were true, then we would also dismiss other Scriptural passages, such as the Magi. Add to that, the Flight to Egypt, the slaughter of the innocents, the Child Jesus in Jerusalem, the adulteress, the raising of Lazarus and many other Scriptural passages.

Then we have other excuses for the denial of the Primacy of Peter. The way it was explained to me is that after Peter pleaded with Jesus to refrain from going to Jerusalem, Jesus said

"get thee behind me Satan" It was explained to me that Jesus had changed his mind.

Do you really believe that?

Was it not that Jesus foretold that deviating from His Destiny was contrary to God's Will? Did Jesus disinherit Peter, or was it a warning the he must follow God's Path?

Following that discourse, what really happened with Peter in his relationship with Jesus? Who did Jesus choose to be present at the Transfiguration? Was it not **Peter**, James and John? And then at Gethsemane, the Agony in the Garden, was it not **Peter,** James, and John? Did not Jesus foretell that Peter would deny Him (Jesus) 3 times before the cock crows? Is there a correlation that denial and Jesus falling 3 times on His way to Calvary? And then was not Jesus successful if fulfilling His Destiny regarding the Crucifixion and Resurrection, and finally His Ascension into Heaven?

Did not Our Lord fortell our weakness by saying that "The Spirit is Willing but the Flesh is Weak"

If Jesus had rejected Peter as the Head of His Church, then why did he say to Peter, "I give to **YOU (Peter)** the <u>Keys to the Kingdom (Heaven)</u>. " Do you really believe that Jesus come down to earth experienced a human existence, His Ministry, His Passion and Crucifixion, Resurrection, and finally His Ascension into Heaven and not establish an Order to fulfill His Ministry. What did Peter experience following the ascension of Jesus into Heaven?

Peter and John were arrested, and when brought before the council was ordered to cease preaching that Christ had risen from the dead. However Peter continued to preach the Word of God. His fame spread, in that many laid at the wayside hoping that his shadow would pass over them and then they would be cured. And many, many were. The blind had their sight restored, and the lame could walk again. He even restored to life, a young girl named Tabitha. While the Apostles followed what they believed to be Jesus directive to go and "teach all Nations", they primarily went among the Jews in various provinces.

A man named Cornelius, a gentile who believed in Jesus, and wished to be His follower, was visited by an Angel and told to go to Peter. Peter was also forewarned by Devine inspiration, that Cornelius would come and the reason why. Peter was to send the Disciples to ALL Nations, and as a result, we gentiles have been accepted into Christ's Family.

Herod had James killed and ordered Peter arrested and imprisoned. His trial was to be held after the Passover, <u>just as Christ's trial was</u>. Peter was bound hand and foot with chains. There were four squads of soldiers of four guards each. There were two guards in his cell and two guards outside his cell door.

During the night an Angel of the of the Lord appeared and cast a spell upon the guards. With that the chains fell from Peter's hands and feet. The cell door opened of itself and Peter and the Angel passed through the prison unseen and unharmed. When Herod heard of Peter's deliverance from the prison, he had the sixteen guards executed. Shortly thereafter, at a State function, Herod dropped dead.

For those who choose to deny the Primacy of Peter, I would ask you, "What did Jesus say". Do you believe that Jesus experienced His human life, His Ministry, His Passion, Crucifixion and Resurrection, only to teach the men of that generation? Or was it to establish His Faith (Church), a Faith to be followed for <u>ALL</u> time? Do you really believe that Jesus returned to Heaven without establishing an Order for His Teaching? Consider the Universe. The Sun, the Moon, the Planets and the Stars. All have a preordained order. Throughout the universe there is order. One can plot exactly where a star or a planet, or a comet was in the past, and where it will be in the future. While, to mortal man, the universe is growing, it is still unchanging. If it is so in the universe, it MUST be in His Church.

Jesus had warned of False Prophets and others who would come and teach in His name. Did not Our Lord say ***"There shall be One Fold and One Shepherd?*** How can there be One Fold when there are well over twenty-five thousand different Protestant Faiths, each one teaching a vastly different Theology.

A theology, that is not only vastly different from the Catholic Church, but also from the Theology of the Founding Fathers of the Reformation.

More of this, in more detail later.

In the past few years, there has been a fad to wear a bracelet with the letters WWJD (What Would Jesus Do) I would ask you, who question of the Primacy of Peter, WDJS (What Did Jesus Say). Was it not:

> **"Thou Art Peter and Upon This Rock I Will Build My Church,**
> **And the Gates of Hell Shall Not Prevail Against It".**

Again, He said to Peter:

> **"I Give to YOU the Keys to the Kingdom of Heaven"**

The last words spoken to Peter, at the Ascension of Jesus, were:

> **"Feed my Lambs, Feed my Sheep".**

For those who still harbor doubts as to the Primacy of Peter, consider Peter's Ministry, and how it parallels that of Our Lord.

Peter restored the sight of the blind, as did Jesus

Peter cured the Lame, even one who was paralyzed from birth, as did Our Lord.

Peter cured a paralyzed man at the doors of the Temple, as did Our Lord

Peter was spirited from the prison, as was our Lord from the mob at the Temple

Peter raised Tabitha from the dead, as Our Lord raised Lazarus

Peter walked on Water, at Our Lord's command; no other Apostle was so honored

Peter suffered Crucifixion, as did Our Lord.

Could this not be Jesus way of bestowing upon Peter the Mantle of Leadership for His Church? As the Universe has a most ridged order, so I believe that Jesus would want a ridged order for His followers and His Teaching?

Some of the reasons that a number of individuals have given me, as to why they either left the Church, or could not join the Church, were that they were told of some wanton act by some Pope several hundreds of years ago.

We have only to look at accusations, by critics of Pope Pius XII, in that they accused him of anti-Semitism, in dealing with the Nazi Holocaust. In reality, he paid millions of dollars to ransom thousands of Jews from the Germans. Hundreds also received sanctuary inside the Vatican.

When Hitler ordered German General Kesselring to take the Jews from the Vatican, the Pope refused to surrender them. The Papal Guards, in their 16th century uniforms and 16th century weapons stood guard outside the Vatican and faced the German Army with its Tiger tanks, and modern weapons.

The German army refused to attack the Pope and the Vatican. As a result, thousands of Jews were saved. This heroic act by the Pope influenced the Chief Rabbi of Rome, to convert to Catholicism. In later years, when there was a celebration for the Pope, the State symphony orchestra of Israel came to Rome to perform for the Pope.

To promote anti-Papacy is just another excuse to seek another religion.

The best way to destroy something is dilute it. A rope is made of many strands, and the best way to break a rope is to break one strand at a time. I would ask, "Has the Protestant movement strengthened the Teachings of Our Lord, or has it

Diluted the Teachings of Jesus?

4

FAITH AND DEEDS

There are several of the Protestant sects that proclaim that Faith alone will save you. Did not Our Lord say, **"Not all who say Lord, Lord will be saved, but only those who do the Will of My Father?** Among the sects that advocate this theology is the Lutheran Church. What lesson should we have learned from the parable of the Talents?

Did not the Master give to the three servants various sums of Talents? They were to guard it for Him, till he returned. What happened when the Master returned? Two of the servants had invested the Talents given to them by the Master, and increased their Talents 100 fold. The third servant took his Talents and buried it in the ground, and returned the Talents to the Master upon His return. The two servants, who invested the Talents given them, were rewarded by the Master. The third servant who buried his Talents was berated by the Master. The third servant said to the master "I *believe* that you are a great and powerful, and I believe that you have mighty powers. I was afraid that I might lose the talents you gave me so I buried them in the ground, so that I might return them to you upon your return."

What was the Masters reply? Was it not that he called the servant "wicked"? Did not the Master berate the servant, saying that IF you believed in me, you would have invested (good deeds) the Talents I gave you, so as to increase my Fold. The servant believed (faith) in the Master, but did not do his bidding (good works), and was therefore condemned.

One explanation I heard regarding "Faith Alone" was that "if" you have Faith you will do Good Works. Is this not a contradiction? The servant said he had faith, but did not use his Talents to increase his Masters Fold. So many of us say we are Christians, and yet we find excuses to ignore Christ's Teaching, or even fail to defend Him.

In the parable of the "Sower of the Seed", Jesus foretold of how those of little faith would fall away. We see that today, in that many, many Souls have left the Church, or refrained from joining the Catholic Church, because of the sex scandal in the Catholic Church. Much ado has been made about it, and rightly so. However, who among us would leave the United States because of the sexual exploits of a Representative, or a Senator, or even the President? All this has happened, but the wrongs do not negate the Constitution. So also the sins of a number of priests or Bishops, or even a Cardinal do not negate the Word of God.

But regarding the priest's sex scandal, in the Words of a noted radio commentator, what is **'the rest of the story"**? Much ado has been made regarding a goodly number of Catholic priests. But according to statistics tabulated by various groups monitoring child abuse by clergy, Catholic priests account for less that one third of the **"reported"** claims, and over two thirds are by Protestant ministers or their staff. I find it somewhat disconcerting that an accusation against a Catholic priest will be given Front Page, while an accusation against a member of the Protestant clergy will be relegated (in the case of the Chicago Tribune) to a small paragraph at the bottom of the Religion page of the Friday edition of the Tribune. This type of reporting of sexual abuse by clergy seems to be the standard for most urban newspapers. Why? While the Catholic Church has paid millions of dollars in compensation, to alleged victims, I have yet to read of any such settlement by any Protestant Church, despite the fact that the incidents of abuse by Protestants outnumber the Catholics by more than two to one.

Could it be that since the Catholic Church is "responsible" for the placement of its clergy, that they are liable for the individual actions of the individual priest? Also the Catholic Church has "a lot of money".

The individual Protestant Churches, for the most part, will hire its own Pastor. The individual church does not have the financial resources that the Catholic Church does, so there is no incentive to prosecute for damages. Also, many of the charges of "misconduct" by clergy are handled in-house in many sects. Very many Protestant Ministers, after being accused of "misconduct", have left their church and gone on to another church. Sometimes, still within the community, and sometimes they will go to another State. However, this is something you will NOT see in many of the urban newspapers.

There are many recorded files regarding these actions, and yet there is very little public notice via our major newspaper publications. I have seen documentation of well over 800 separate cases of sexual abuse by Protestant clergy and their staff, and I would ask you how many of these charges have you seen in our major daily newspapers?

How many of you know of a Protestant clergy, has been "dismissed" from one congregation, and then goes to another and then commits the same heinous acts against young boys.

The latest findings, on sexual abuse of minors reveal that up to 10% of public school children are victims of sexual abuse. Where is the outrage? We seem to ONLY hear of sexual abuse by Catholic priests.

Sexual abuse of minors by Protestant Clergy
Baptist ministers 147
"Bible" Church Ministers 251
Anglican / Episcopal priests 140
Lutheran Ministers 38
Methodist Ministers 46
Presbyterian Ministers 19
Various Church Ministers 197

This is accordance with Title 17 U.S.C. Section 107 reformation.com

This is NOT a complete list as, many "store front" churches would have handled this problem privately. Millions of dollars have been awarded to victims of Protestant sexual abuse, but very little of this "news" is published in the Mail line media. Both Catholic priests and Protestant clergy who have perpetrated these heinous acts should ALL be punished, and removed from ministry.

Where I find fault with the Catholic Church and the various Protestant Churches is in what I consider ignoring the "root" cause of most abuses. The Churches and the media all call it "sexual child abuse" and the perpetrator is classified as a pedophile.

What is a pedophile? Is it not a person that sexually abused children? Boys and girls. The VAST, VAST majority of the "reported" claims of sexual abuse are related to sex between men and boys. When a person has sex with another person of the same sex, is it not considered a homosexual act? Are not those who commit a homosexual act considered homosexuals?

What do you call a man who has sex with dozens and dozens of very young boys and young men? Is not the perpetrator a homosexual? So here we come to another option being taken by the "Cafeteria" Christians.

5

Homosexuality

A growing number of Main Line Protestant Churches and many "Store Front" churches, in an effort to bolster their congregation, are advocating acceptance of the homosexual life style. Today it is call an "alternative life style". Some Churches have gone so far as to ordain these individuals as ministers and Bishops. Among this group of Churches are the Anglican / Episcopalian, the Lutheran, and the United Methodist, and a goodly number of Nondenominational Churches.

Several years ago, I had occasion to hear a minister from the Broadway United Methodist Church, in Chicago, give an excuse for his thinking, regarding performing a wedding for homosexual couples. Rev Gregory Dell appeared on the Spike O'Dell radio show on station WGN (720).

My understanding of what the Rev had to say regarding homosexuality was, that he did agree that Scripture does say that for *"a man to lay with a man, as with a woman, is an abomination"*.(sin) However, Rev Dell said, that Scripture mandated "stoning.", and this is not acceptable today. So in his thoughts (in my understanding) since stoning is incompatible with modern living, the sin is therefore nullified.

This attitude seems to prevail in the Episcopal Faith also. Newly elected (2006) Bishop Katherine Janet Schori, has expounded the theory that since we, modern man, have ignored the prohibition regarding food and drink, as related in the Old

Testament, we can therefore ignore or deny the prohibition regarding homosexuality.

To me these are the most lame brained, stupidest excuse I have ever heard. If then, we are to accept these premises, we must of necessity, then accept incest as an ordinary way of life, for does it not call for the same punishment? Then what of murder? Does not Scripture call for terminal punishment? And what of adultery? Does not Scripture call for the same punishment as homosexuality?

How did Jesus confront this problem?

When the adulteress was brought before Jesus, He was asked to pass judgment on her. What was His judgment? Was it go and enjoy yourself, because the punishment is too extreme? Or did He admonish her to go and not get caught again? What did He say? I firmly believe that Jesus said:

Go, and SIN no more

The SIN still exists.

It is my belief that the Methodist Church is involved with a "Bait and Switch" method of Theology. While the Methodist Church does not condone same sex marriage, they have applied the ploy of "if you can't get in the front door, then go in by the back door". It appears that Bishop Anne Sherer of Omaha, Nebraska, approved a policy adopted by the Methodist Church on May 7th, 2006. The policy stated, (to my understanding) that while the Methodist Church does not allow for same sex marriages, any couple that are married in another Faith, will be welcome in the Methodist Faith as married couples. Bishop said that "all are welcome". As a minister of God, her admonition should be for the same sex couples, to refrain from sexual intercourse. I did not note that in her statement.

Several Methodist ministers I have known of are applying that procedure to homosexual couples. They will either marry them outside the church, or refer them to another Faith that condones same sex marriage, and then welcoming the homosexual couple into their Faith, without restricting their sexual proclivities.

Here it appears that the Methodist (to me) is involved in a "bait and switch" theology. I have heard of a Methodist Minister, in North Chicago, who has advocated the acceptance of same sex marriage, but when forbidden by his Church, advocated marrying the "couple" outside the Church and then welcoming them into the Congregation.

This is a bit confusing to me. If the Methodist Faith condemns homosexual marriage, how then can it accept the marriage of same sex couples from another Faith? Like the Presbyterian with the quasi acceptance of icons of the Blessed Virgin in some churches, in order to gain converts, it would appear that the Methodists are utilizing the same "bait and switch" methods.

Now coming back to the Anglicans, Bishop Robert Duncan, of Pittsburg, warned that failure to act, by Rowan Williams, Arch Bishop of Canterbury, on the growing schism within the Anglican community, would be detrimental to the Church.

My personal belief is that the situation that confronts Arch Bishop Rowan Williams, is like that of former United States President James Buchanan. Buchanan, like Arch Bishop Williams, was faced with a serious dilemma. Failure to act by Buchanan, resulted in several States in the Union, seceding, and forming a new nation. *The Confederate States of America.* The result was a bloody Civil War. Actions by President Lincoln, resulted in the reunification of all the States, of what is today, the United States of America.

Arch Bishop Rowan William, like Buchanan, seems incapable of wielding the authority of his office. A sign of his theological impendence, was ignoring (what I consider) the heresy by an Episcopalian priest, who later was ordained as a Bishop in the Anglican Communion. The heresy was that the priest (an avowed homosexual) who abandoned his wife and children, for a male lover, declared that Jesus was a homosexual. This declaration by Rev Robinson has been followed by a nondenominational female minister who also subscribes to this belief. In my opinion, unless Arch Bishop Williams acts as the dynamic leader he should be, the result will be the formation of another "Christian" sect. A sect that will see a further erosion of Scripture.

To my personal belief, for not only the Anglican Communion and the Protestant movement, in general, to stand mute, in the face of these heresies, is quasi approval of the heresy.

I just cannot imagine a Catholic Pope, or a Moslem Imam remaining mute, as does Arch Bishop Williams, and not take some form of action regarding this statement of heresy. In matter of fact, the whole Protestant community is standing mute on this heresy. Not a single Protestant theologian has refuted this heresy. With the Pope, the penalty most probably would be excommunication. With the Moslems, the penalty could be execution.

Scripture gives us the lesson regarding homosexuality in the experience of Lot and his family.

Sodom and Gomorrah.

Why were these cities destroyed? Was it not because of the "life style"? What happened when the two Angels came to warn Lot? Did not the men of the city come to Lot, and demand of him, that he give them the two men in his home? Even though Lot offered his two virgin daughters in exchange, they still demanded the two men in the house, so they could use them as a man uses a woman.

Through the powers of the Angels, Lot and his wife and two daughters were spirited from the city, which was then destroyed by fire and brimstone. It was if the two cities had been destroyed by an atomic bomb. Evidence today, indicates that something atomic destroyed the area. Plus the fact that recent archeological findings are that there were well over a million graves, with indications that the inhabitants before the cataclysm were well fed. But today, nothing grows in that area.

Is the world facing another such calamity? It is my belief that this is what we are faced with now. And it is the AIDS epidemic. What are the seeds? Is it not the homosexual life style?

In 1981, a new and deadly virus was discovered. Originally, they called it Homosexual pneumonia. That was, because of the first 41 cases reported; all 41 victims were homosexual men. The homosexual community railed against the Center for Disease Control and the government, because of what they perceived as lack of action due to prejudice against homosexuals.

Those 41 original cases of AIDS have now mushroomed into well over 80 million people, and still no cure in sight. Scientist will admit that there are many, many individual who are <u>unaware</u> that they have the infection. Third world Countries have a most inadequate health system, and very many cases go unreported. The President of South Africa denies that AIDS exists. He blames the problem on malnutrition. China, India, Saudi Arabia and others are now beginning to accept the FACT that their Countries have been exposed to the AIDS virus.

AIDS is very easily prevented. All one has to do, is live a life that God had ordained. No fornication, No adultery, No drugs, and living a committed heterosexual married life.

Originally the homosexual community tried to show that they were not responsible for the spread of the virus. They pointed out several heterosexuals who had contracted the virus. But it was proven that many homosexuals lead a double life. That the average homosexual has, over a period of time, eight different partners. Many of these partners have led a double life, and is so doing have infected their spouse or their girlfriend. In many cases it is both, wife and girl friend. These in turn, have infected their lovers. Many homosexuals are drug addicts, and in sharing their needles, they have in turn infected others.

The homosexual community tried to "prove" that the virus contamination could come from another source. They cited a case of a young lad named Ryan White who had been infected with the virus. He was a lad, with no sexual experience, and not a drug addict. But then it was proven that Ryan had been given infected blood, during a transfusion.

Once again the homosexual community tried to show that there was another source for the spread of the infection. They pointed to a case in Florida of a young virgin that was diagnosed with AIDS. She also was not a drug user. But, here again, it was proven that she was deliberately infected by her dentist, who had full blown AIDS. Not only had he infected Kimberly, but several other patients as well.

Many deceased American Negros, have a death certificate that cites the cause of death as a drug overdose, when in reality it is AIDS. In denying the existence of AIDS, very many Black women are being infected. This is caused by the Negro mentality, that it is better to be a drug addict than a homosexual. As a result, over 50% of the new cases of HIV are among Negro men, and close to 25% of Negro women.

Here in the United States, Homosexuals and drug addicts comprise a small minority of the population, but they account for close to 75 % of all the AIDS infections.

China, which a few years ago, reported about a thousand cases of AIDS, now admits to well over one million infections. The same is true of India. Moslem countries are reluctant to report anything regarding AIDS.

The United States alone has pledged 15 Billion dollars to fight AIDS. Yet, again, it cost nothing <u>to prevent AIDS</u>. Not One Red Cent. Just live according to God's Laws. A monogamous, heterosexual life. Spending Billions of dollars on AIDS prevention and research, without attacking the root cause, is akin to a group of people in a leaking boat, spending all their time trying to bail out the leaking boat and doing nothing about the cause of the leak. The cause is (in my opinion) an immoral illegal life style.

AIDS is 99.44% preventable.

The 15 Billion dollars we are committed to spend on AIDS research, could instead, **GIVE**, 75 thousand families a new house, furnished with essentials , including TV, VCR, freezer, refrigerator, furniture, etc, etc, plus a brand new automobile. All to try and help people who are self destructing, and could, with a little effort on their part be safe from the AIDS virus.

What I find most distressing is that if I walk down any street in the United States, with a loaded gun, hidden in my jacket, I could be arrested. But, an individual, who has the AIDS virus, IS

PROTECTED by the HIPPA laws. Yet these individuals can, and do, have indiscriminate sex, and infect countless individual, who intern infect others with an **incurable disease**.

Already there is a movement, within not only the United States, but also Canada, to legalize polygamy. The reasoning is that if the United States or Canada is to accept one diverse life style, they MUST accept the other. There have been protest marches in both countries advocating polygamy.

Not to be undone, NAMBLA is advocating vacating the Laws regarding sex between "consenting" men and *minor* boys. There are hundreds Of Clubs, catering to this perversion. In accepting the homosexual life style, as many Faiths and politicians seem bent on doing, they are opening a Pandora's Box, and we can all see what will then transpire.

6

MARIONALOGY

Which of the Protestant sects openly preach against fornication? Many of these same sects openly preach against the Mother of Jesus, and condemn Catholics for honoring Her. There was a time, not too long ago that virginity was looked upon as a state of grace. Today a virgin is looked upon as an aberration. One who is not with the *times*.

What do we see on our televisions today, or in our movies? Bed hopping! It seems that only the Catholic Church was voiced disapproval of this type of entertainment.

In the 1950's there was an international outcry, regarding a 10 year old girl giving birth to a baby. Today, as a result of the "Sexual Revolution", fornication has been an accepted way of life. This in return has resulted in thousands of children bearing children. It is no longer an anomaly, but an accepted fact of life. Daily we hear of 10, 11, and 12, year old girls having babies. *Babies having babies*!

One third of babies born today, in the United States, are to unwed mothers. This coupled with the fact that 25% of women of child bearing age are infected with a sexually transmitted disease. In times past, these diseases were referred as Venereal Disease. Many of these infections are incurable. Some render a female sterile. Some threaten her life.

Most Protestant sects, advocate condoms as a method of practicing "safe sex". This is tantamount to playing "Russian Roulette", by removing 9 of the 10 bullets in the gun. While condoms are *safer* then "unprotected" sex, they still present a distinct probability of spreading infection, and also have resulted in pregnancy. The condom failure rate is from 7 to 10% of the time.

Then we come to abortions. Millions of babies have been slaughtered in the past 20 years here in the USA. Abortion has become a rule, rather than the exception. In the animal kingdom, the mother would fight to the death to protect her cub. Today's woman disposed her progeny as one disposes of trash. A sad commentary of today's society. If the Protestant Churches would join the Catholic Church in protesting this aberration, the lives of countless babies would be saved.

Scripture has recorded two other episodes of "slaughter of the innocents". At the time of Moses and after the birth of Jesus.

Many defenders of abortion "claim" that it is necessary to save the life of the mother. What a fallacy! There are more women dieing in automobile accidents than in child birth. Yet we do not prohibit women from riding in cars. More women die from drug over dose, than in child birth. At age 21 days, a baby (fetus) has a heart beat. It is a living, growing human being, yet it is killed and thrown into the garbage, like so much trash.

Imagine if you will, if an individual were on life support, and had a beating heart, and a functional respiratory system plus its internal systems were improving, and had a 99.44% chance of a healthy survival, if <u>left on "life support,"</u> and that life support was terminated, would you not call that act, of termination, **murder**. My personal belief is that anyone involved in the termination of a viable life, should be charged with murder. The mother, the doctor, the nurse, plus those that facilitate the crime, should be charged with abetting the act.

Jesus said, of the little children:
> **"Of such is the Kingdom of Heaven."**

He also said:

"He who harms the least of my little ones, it would be better for him if a

Mill stone were tied about his neck and he be thrown into the deep."

Much hue and cry is made when the State is about to execute a convicted felon. A felon who had a trial, and was found guilty. A felon who had an appeal, after an appeal, and after even more appeals, and was found guilty of the crime. And still mobs of "well wishers", will protest the death of the felon. Yes I do agree that sometimes, an innocent individual will be convicted and executed. Most of the felon so convicted, are guilty, and do deserve the severe punishment. With the "unborn", they are ALL innocent, and yet they are executed. At least the felon is buried with dignity. The fetus (baby) is discarded in the trash. Ask an expectant mother how her "fetus" is doing and she will be insulted. *It is a baby*! To the mother it is a baby. A living, growing part of her.

No where in the universe is there anything remotely resembling the human race. Life on Earth is a Miracle, from God. Who is there to speak for the unborn, besides the Catholic Church?

To me, the root source of the denigration of virginity and the quasi acceptance of abortion lay with the Neo Protestant theology of rejection of Mary, the "Blessed Virgin".

While most Protestant Faiths will admit that Jesus was born of a virgin, most will teach that His mother had several children at a later time. But then again, some sects will state that the "children" mentioned in Scripture as brothers and sisters of Jesus, were in fact children from Joseph's first wife. Protestantism in incapable of ONE Teaching. Most Protestant Faiths will accuse the Catholic Church of deifying Her.

One of the explanations I have heard from my Protestant friends regarding The Virginity of Mary is the word "Charis" in scripture. They had pointed out that the Angel Gabriel's greeting to Mary was "Highly Favored One". As, to them, "Charis" means highly favored, not "Full of Grace" as us Catholics believe.

What they fail to acknowledge is that in the rest of Scripture, "Charis" is interpreted as "Full of Grace", just as

Catholics believe. It is ONLY in this one passage that Charis is interpreted as "highly Favored", the rest of Scriptural interpretations are "Full of Grace".

I had asked many Protestant Faiths if they were cognizant of any member of the Faith, having been "visited" by either a Saint or the Blessed Virgin. Not one member of a Protestant Faith is recorded as having been visited by the Blessed Virgin Mary.

What then of Her reported visits to Catholics?

St James and the Virgin Mary

The Blessed Virgin has been reported to have been seen several times. At least once shortly after her death. The Apostle James, reported to have seen her, when he was in what is now Saragossa, Spain, in 40 A D, and reported the apparition to the Queen. Upon his return to Jerusalem, in 44 A D, James was killed by Herod.

Here we have an Apostle of Christ, reporting the apparition. There is a Cathedral built upon the spot where Saint James reported the Vision of Mary, the Mother of Jesus.

Three very prominent events accrued in historical times. One in Mexico. One in France. And one in Portugal. There were several others, but the Church leaves to the faithful, to accept or deny the other events.

Our Lady of Tepeyac

With the apparitions in Mexico, France and Portugal, there is visible evidence that miracles took place.

In 1531, a Mexican peasant, claimed to have been "visited" by a most beautiful Lady. She told him to go to the Bishop, and tell him she requested a Cathedral be built. The Bishop doubted the young man, and told him, if there were such a person, she should give him Castilian roses. Roses of that type were not growing at that time of the year. Yet Juan Diego found the roses on the hill top, enclosed them in his tilma (cloak), and took them to the

Bishop. Upon opening the tilma, there was embossed upon the tilma, a picture of a beautiful woman surrounded by roses.

Many have tried to debunk this apparition. Some claim there was no such person as Juan Diego. Well that is like the detractors who claim that Paul Revere did not make the famous ride on April 18th 1775, to warn the Colonists of the approaching British soldiers. Perhaps Paul did not make the "ride", but the event of the "ride" and the outcome is an historical fact. The result of the "ride" was *the shot* that was heard around the World. It was the beginning of Democracy. The power for people to choose their own government.

As a direct result of the apparition, the Aztecs were converted to Christianity (Catholicism). The Virgin Mary (Our Lady of Tepeyac) had become the patron Saint of Mexico.

One attempt was made to replicate the tilma, with "paintings" of the figure of Mary embossed on the tilma along with the drawings of the roses. The normal life expectancy of a tilma is less than 20 years. The original tilma, can be seen today at the cathedral in Mexico. It has not deteriorated in the least. For over one hundred and sixty years it was exposed to the all elements. The Sun, heat, dampness, smoke from the candles, and all effect of the environment.

Two duplicate tilmas were hung in the same environment , and in less than nine years they were completely corrupted by the elements. Yet the original tilma, withstood the same elements for over 160 years. Even an attempted bombing, while destroying the structure around the tilma, did not so much as scratch it.

The cathedral is festooned with relics and notes of individual who have been a recipient of a miracle through the intercession of the Blessed Mother.

Our Lady of Lourdes

In 1858, there was a report of our Blessed Mother, by three very young children. The eldest, *Bernadette Soubirous age 14* shortly after receiving her first communion, reported that she had seen a very beautiful woman, who said she was the Immaculate Conception. When the children were asked if they new what that phrase meant, the children replied they did not.

Church authorities, and civil authorities, warned the children that they would be severely punished if they did not recant their claim of seeing the "beautiful Lady". The children refused to recant, despite the pleas from their parents and demands by Church and civil authorities.

The superintendent of police, then said that if this "Lady" would provide a miracle, then they could believe in Her. By digging in the ground, with her bare hands, a spring burst forth. Still not satisfied, the police wanted more proof. This was fulfilled by immersing an infant child, paralyzed from birth into the pool formed by the spring. Upon returning the child from the pool, the child's paralysis was found to be cured.

There have been hundreds of miraculous cures attributed to the Virgin Mary at Lourdes. While hundreds have been documented by medical records, thousands of others do claim that they have been blessed by the Virgin Mary, and all sorts of illness have been cured. Cancer, heart problems, T.B., paralyses of all sorts, have been cured. No Protestant edifice can make a similar claim.

Twenty years after Bernadette died, the Catholic Church, took steps to canonize her as a Saint. Before a person can be declared a Saint, A miracle MUST be documented. There were several miracles attributed to Bernadette. However, when her body was exhumed from her grave, it was found to be uncorrupted. The condition of the body was as if she had just "passed away". All other bodies in the cemetery were all decayed. Only Bernadette's body was uncorrupted. Today, you can visit the convent at Lourdes and view her body, which is now encased in a glass case.

The Blessed Mother Mary told Bernadette that she (Bernadette) would suffer greatly in her mortal life, but would find joy in Heaven. Bernadette did indeed suffer greatly in her short life. She died at a very early age.

Our Lady of Fatima

In 1917, at Fatima Portugal, Our Lady appeared to three preteen children. When the children told of the apparition, they were dismissed as foolish children. However, Lucia the eldest (10 years old) insisted that a very beautiful woman appeared to them in the open field.

Both Church and civic authorities warned the children not to spread such stories. Still they persisted. Finally, the village police took them into custody and taking each child separately told that they would be tortured if they did not recant. Despite the harsh treatment, the children again persisted in their story of the Beautiful Lady.

Finally, the children were asked what the Lady had told them. They replied that the Lady told them that the world must pray for the return of Russia to Christianity. If Russia did not, then a very terrible event would take place that would destroy millions of lives.

One must remember that at this very time, Russia was a beaten nation. It had been humiliated by Japan 15 years previous, and had just surrendered to the Central Powers in World War I. Also, Russia was in the early stages of a revolution. It was difficult to believe that Russia could be a threat to anyone.

Those of us in the Catholic Church had been asked to pray for the conversion of Russia.

Anyone who has lived through the 30's to the 90's along with the Cold War does know the threat that Russia possessed. Tens of millions of souls perished. It was universally believed that the only power to bring an end to the Communist rule would be atomic power. We all believed there would be another war involving the use of atomic bombs.

Many of us will remember the confrontation before the Russian White House, when the Communist Party officials demanded that Boris Yeltsin and his government surrender. Tanks and troops surrounded the White House. Mobs of *unarmed peasants* also were there to lend moral support and to

PRAY to God for deliverance from the Communists. One shot! One single shot would have lead to a devastating blood bath. Instead, the Russian troops, to a man, refused to fire.

Russian had returned to Christianity, and the Cold War ended.

Sister Lucia lived to see beginning of the Communist menace, dominated by anti Christians where belief in God was a violation of State law and could and did result in prison. She also lived to see the power of prayer, through the Blessed Mother Mary, bring about the downfall of the Soviet Union.

In order to dissuade throngs of pilgrims who were flocking to Fatima, the authorities wanted a tangible sign to prove the Lady exists. The authorities were told that at noon the following day, the Lady would produce a miracle.

The following day dawned with an overcast sky and misting rain falling. Precisely at noon, a sign in the Heavens appeared. The sign was witnessed by thousands of people and also the news media. It appeared that the Sun was dancing in the sky, and then there appeared, what was believed to be a huge Cross in the sky. The Cross was seen as far away as the battle fields in Flanders, Belgium. Despite the drizzling rain, after the apparition, everyone was dry. There was no mud.

In later years, astronomers announced that the "cross" seen in the sky from Fatima, Portugal, to the battle field in Northern France, was in reality a Nova (star) that had exploded several thousands of "light" years ago.

The children gave the authorities another prediction. Two of the children would die in very early childhood, and would join the Beautiful Lady in Heaven. Two did die within two years. The last one, Lucia became a Nun and lived into her 90's. She was visited by all the reigning Popes during her life time. She also warned Pope John Paul II that an attempt would be made on his life.

An attempt was made (*on the anniversary of the first apparition at Fatima*) on the life of Pope John Paul II. He severely wounded, but did survive. John Paul II was instrumental in helping to bring about the down fall of Communist Russia. It is ironic, that the only shot involved in bringing about the down fall of the Soviet Union (Russia), was an attempt to kill the man instrumental in its demise.

Here we have three sub teen children, not only prophesying the death of two of them, but the cataclysm that the Soviet Union (Russia) would propel upon the World, and add to that the attempt to assassinate a Pope, and last but not least, "guessing" (prophesying) when a Nova that exploded thousands of years ago, would become visible at the exact moment that the "Beautiful" Lady told them.

If this is pure luck, then I would love to have those kids in Las Vegas. It has to either luck, or the "hand of God". I go for the latter.

NO Protestant Faith has ever had any similar manifestation.

The Blessed Virgin has appeared many times to the Faithful. With most apparitions there is documented viable proof that something of a most extraordinary nature took place.

Miracles happen every day. When you consider what is involved in the birth of a child , it can only be considered a miracle. Where else in the universe does this happen? Perhaps I am most fortunate in that I do believe that I and my family have experienced not one, but several miracles.

At age 18 months, the doctor gave me 6 hours to live. He said I would not see the sunrise. Yet, here I am more that 80 years later. In 1943, the Army doctors rejected me as unfit for military service. Limited service also rejected me because they said I have a bad heart. My family doctor said they were wrong. Yet Army doctors in 1943 and again in 1951 (Korean War) all said I had a bad heart. Yet when I took an exam for a private pilot's license, I was giving a clean "bill of health". There are other incidences, where by for the Grace of God, I should have been killed.

My "future" wife was of very slight build. While standing on the El platform in downtown Chicago one very windy wintry day, she was push by a strong wind, and just as she was about to fall upon the El tracks, before an oncoming train, two individuals grabbed each of her arms and brought her to safety. As she turned to thank them, there was no one in sight. Angels?

In 1957, we had just adopted a baby girl. At age 4 months she developed a very high fever, 105-106, and was unable to retain any nourishment. We were afraid to take her to the hospital as we thought that the Adoption agency (Catholic Charities) would think of us as unfit parents, and take the baby from us. Many friends and relatives gave us remedies to combat this malady. We did not use any of them, but decided that the life of the baby was more important than our own vanity, and we prepared to take her to the hospital.

The child's aunt arrived and asked to bless her with oil from the Shrine of Saint Anne (*the mother of the Blessed Virgin Mary*). Within mere minutes the fever broke and the baby was able to take nourishment.

In later years, we went on a pilgrimage to the Shrine of St Anne, in Quebec, Canada. At the Shrine we view **thousand of crutches festooning the many pillars** of the church. We also viewed and read some of the thousands of letters of recipients of, what they believed, as we believe, was indeed an intercession (miracle) by the Blessed Virgin.

All of the apparitions have appeared to very young and very religious individuals. All defied authorities. All were threatened with torture. All defied the civic authorities, the Church authorities, and even their parents.

Why is it that no Protestant has been blessed by a "visit" from the Blessed Virgin, the Mother of our Lord? In each apparition, the Blessed Mother appeals for us to bring souls to **Her Son, Jesus Christ**.

To quote the words of one of the **founders** of the **Reformation:**

> **"To deny the Perpetual Virginity of Mary,
> and her Immaculate Conception
> is to deny the Divinity of Jesus Christ."**

This quote is from a Founder of the Reformation. We will have more on this later. Much more will be said regarding the beliefs of the Founding Fathers of the Reformation, and the contradictory Theology of their followers.

Many of us have been blessed with miracles, but we do not realize it. There is an expression, that "they can't see the forest for the trees". So it is in most lives. God sends us a Blessing (miracle) and we look at it as lucky happenstance. Someone would have to live the experiences I just related to get a full appreciation of them. We have lived it, and felt it, and believe it, that we were <u>Blessed for some Special Purpose</u>.

The complaint of most people, regarding miracles, is if *"they don't see it, they can't believe it"*. They also say that miracles happened many centuries ago, but not today. Yet, they have happened, and do happen in our time.

The problem is one that is similar to St Thomas. "Unless I see, I cannot believe" What did Our Lord say?

Blessed are they who have not seen, and yet believe.

One other aspect of the Anti Marian agenda by Protestants is that Catholics "pray" to her. They seem to believe that we Catholics are deifying her. Nothing could be further from the Truth. The most common from of prayer to Mary is in the "Hail Mary" and also is an interregnal part of the rosary.

What then, of the rosary? First there is the Act of Faith, which many Protestant sects also use, completely overlooking the mention of: "I believe in the Holy Catholic Church." Etc. There also is the "Our Father", which most Protestant Faith prays. Then there is the "Hail Mary". Let us look at the "Hail Mary".

"Hail Mary, full of Grace, the Lord is with thee".

Now I ask you, what is wrong with that? Is this not the greeting that the Arch Angel Gabriel gave to the young virgin?

Are we wrong to repeat what God had instructed the Angel to say? I think not.

"Blessed are you among Women, and Blessed is the fruit of thy womb, Jesus".

Now, tell me what is wrong with that saying (prayer)? Is not the "fruit" of Her womb, Jesus, and should He not be Blessed? In this prayer to Mary, we are honoring God.

**"Holy Mary, Mother of God, *pray for us sinners*,
Now and at the hour of our death, Amen."**

Here is the prayer we Catholics pray to the Mother of Jesus (God) and in so doing we are asking Her to *intercede* for us with Her Heavenly Son, Jesus Christ, and asking Her *to pray for us*. . Tell me where we could possibly be wrong with this prayer.

7

Stigmata

There are many individual who have been Blessed with the Stigmata of Christ's wounds. In my research I have found that from the time of St Francis of Assisi in1224 the first to receive the stigmata, to today there are over 230 records of individuals who have "suffered" the Stigmata.

Some psychiatrists believe that this "condition" is caused by an extreme emotional experience. Of the over 230 Stigmatics, I found that ALL were of the Catholic Faith. There may be others from other Faiths, but I have been unable to find them.

In my lifetime I know of three individuals who were "Blessed" with the Stigmata. One was Theresa Neumann, in Germany. She would experience the Stigmata on Fridays, and it would generally last until Sunday. Another was Padre Pio, who bled from the wounds of Christ for over 40 years. The third was a very young girl in Worcester, Massachusetts.

On Good Friday, in 1996, Audrey Santo a twelve year old child, brain damaged since she was 3 years old, experienced the Stigmata. There have been other incidents of a miraculous nature which has resulted in several of her nurses converting to Catholicism

When it was discovered that Padre Pio was so afflicted, he was ordered, by the Pope, to go to a monastery, and NOT to promote his stigmata. He was allowed to say daily Mass, and to hear confessions. He was also ordered not to write or speak of his experience in public. Yet his fame spread. Many would come to him for confession. In the confessional, he would tell *you* your sins.

On one occasion, he confronted a man who came to give his confession. Parde Pio told the man that "his" confession was a sham. His intention was to kill his wife, and deflect any suspicion about him, as he had just rejoined the Church. The man fled the confessional in panic, but later returned and confessed to Padre Pio, that indeed he had intended to kill his wife. He begged Padre Pio for forgiveness, and promised that he would amend his life.

The Masses given by Padre Pio were over two hours long, and participating in the Mass was a very moving experience. Many miracles were recorded in his name. A blind girl received her sight when she received "Holy" communion from the Padre. Another, a worker helping to build the hospital at the monastery was injured by a premature explosion. The doctors said his eyes were damaged beyond repair, as stone fragments were imbedded in his eyes. When Padre Pio blessed him, he told the man, that every thing would be all right and upon removing the bandages, his eyes were back to normal.

A family friend had written to Padre Pio, and asked him to pray for her husband, as he had just had a physical examination, and the doctor told him that he had an incurable blood disease. Padre Pio wrote back that there was nothing physically wrong with her husband, and that he should get a second opinion from another doctor. Indeed, the second test proved that there was no physical problem.

The head of the Communist Party, in Italy, came to the monastery, in an attempt to expose Padre Pio as a fraud. Instead, after visiting with the Padre, the man renounced Communism and converted to Catholicism. To recite all of the miracles attributed to Padre Pio would take a complete book.

All of the bandages that were removed from the Padre daily were sent to Rome. There are several recorded cases were relics of the bandages were sent, by Rome, to selected individuals. The result has been miraculous cures from cancer and diabetes among many other cures.

When Padre suffered a hernia that required an operation, he asked the doctor to promise to refrain from examining his Stigmata, while he was sedated. The doctor told him that he could not make and keep such a promise. Padre Pio then opted to have the operation without anesthesia. As a result from the pain from the surgery the Padre "passed" out. At which time the doctor did examined the Stigmata, and found that indeed there was a blood like substance emanating from the wounds, wounds similar to the wounds of the crucifixion. The wound from the hernia operation healed as any normal operation scar would heal. However the wounds of the Stigmata continue to emanate blood for over 40 years.

Padre Pio was asked by Pope John Paul II to pray for a dear friend of his, from his days in the Polish underground. The woman had just given birth to her first child, and the doctors' informed her husband that she had a cancer and that she would be dead inside of three months. Four months later, the doctors were amazed to find that there was no cancer.

Was it a miracle? Was it through the intervention of Padre Pio? I think so.

Padre Pio was canonized a Saint in the Catholic Church in the shortest possible time. This has been due to the very many miracles attributed to him.

Many skeptics have tried to debunk the experiences of Juan Diego, Bernadette, Lucia , Padre Pio and Theresa Neumann. All have failed, and in many instances have they themselves been converted to Catholicism. Several of those converted as a result of their experience with Theresa Neumann, suffered martyrdom in defending their new found faith, during the Nazi regime.

Theresa Neumann was a young farm girl in Konnersreuth, Germany. Her desire was to become a Nun and to do missionary work in Africa. However, in 1918, while helping to put out a fire at a neighbors farm, Theresa suffered an injury to her spine that left her cripple and bedridden. She then lost her sight, so that she could no longer walk or see.

Theresa never questioned her fate, and the pain and suffering she experienced. Theresa had a great affinity for Saint Therese Lisieux, (the Little Flower). Theresa had prayed to her from a prayer card she had, and one day five years after the accident, Theresa dreamt that someone was touching her pillow. She opened her eyes and realized that she could now see. Is it a Miracle or work of the Devil? Theresa was still crippled, but at least she could see.

Two years after the return of her sight, it became evident that, due to the injury to her leg, it must be amputated. Her mother was very much against the amputation. A rose petal was obtained, that had touched a relic of the "Little Flower" (St Therese) and it was placed on her injured leg. When the bandages were removed, her leg was healthy. Was this the work of the Devil, or a Miracle from God through St Therese? Theresa was able to see and now to walk.

Theresa did not explain to her parents what had really occurred. She met with her parish priest and explained to him what had occurred. Theresa Neumann told her priest that St Therese had come to her and asked Theresa Neumann what she wanted. Theresa replied that she wanted to serve her Savior. St Therese told her that she would walk and see, but she would suffer for the glory of *bringing Souls to Christ*. Theresa replied that she only wanted to be able to serve her Savior.

Shortly thereafter, Theresa was marked by our Lords stigmata. This appeared almost every Friday and left her on Sunday. She experienced this phenomenon for over twenty years. That however was not the end of the miracle. What happened after is;

"The rest of the story".

As a result of the stigmata, Theresa no longer partook of food or drink, except for a few sips of water after she received the host at Holy Communion. For twenty years she had not eaten food or drink liquids. Needless to say, very many doubted her, even the Catholic Church. Finally she was asked to submit to an extensive examination.

It was asked that she be placed in a neighboring village hospital, and that she be under observation for twenty four hours a day for fifteen days. The doctors had decided on a fifteen day period of observation, because their belief was that the human body cannot survive without food or drink for that period of time.

Visitors were not allowed, and there were at least four doctors or nurses **with her at all times.** She was not given any intravenous fluid or any medication. During the fifteen day of observation, she neither defecated nor urinated. Her only sustenance was, as it already had been, daily reception of the Holy Eucharist followed by a few "sips" of water.

Her father was displeased that the staff, observing his daughter was comprised of many Protestants. However this is as it should have been. Had there been no Protestant doctors or nurses, then the entire procedure would have been suspect. However, after the examination, several of the doctors and nurses did convert to Catholicism.

In 2005 there were news reports of a Buddhist youth who had not eaten for six months. The difference here is that no one was allowed to come within 160 feet of him, and his handlers were all Buddhist priests. He could only be seen for twelve hours a day, and his staff, unlike the staff that observed Theresa, was all Buddhists. Theresa was observed twenty four hours a day, by impartial, observers, not by priests or Nuns. The international scientific community pressed for a close examination of the lad. When thus pressed, the Buddhist boy and his "handlers" disappeared. A year has passed and there has been no word as to where he is today.

Theresa Neumann did submit to a medical examination by independent doctors and nurses for twenty four hours a day, for fifteen days. Doctors and nurses of a different religious persuasion were all part of the staff.

With Theresa Neumann we have verified medical records, detailing her blindness, her crippling spine injury, and her injured leg that her doctors wanted to amputate. There is the rose petal that had touched the relic of St Therese "the Little

Flower", having been placed on the injured leg, which resulted in an instantaneous cure

Among the other phenomenal acts by Theresa Neumann, was that she would look at strangers and know whether they were Catholic or Protestant. She said that Catholics had a "glow" about them. She was give another test, in which she was in an enclosed auto and driven through several towns. She would then note that they were passing a Catholic Church, even though see could not see outside the auto. She was correct 100% of the time.

Protestants condemn Catholics for praying to a Saint to intercede on their behalf, with Our Lord. Yet all of these petitions resulted in the greater Glory of Jesus Christ.

Many skeptics came to Padre Pio and Theresa Neumann, in an effort to "expose" them as frauds. None could, and in turn, many were converted to Catholicism. Was this the "works" of the Devil? Or was it actions by Saints to bring about the greater Glory of Jesus Christ?

8

THE PROTESTANT BIBLE

What I find most interesting is that for the most part, all Protestant denominations us the King James Version of the Bible. Humor me for a moment. Let us compare the Protestant Bible with the United States Bible, the *Constitution*.

In the Protestant Movement we have the Mainline Faiths. There are the Lutherans, Anglicans, Episcopalians, Methodists, Presbyterians, and a few others. Then there are the Nondenominational Faiths, and also the "store front" faiths. Compare this with the United States. We have the States themselves and then there are the Counties, followed by the Townships.

With the Protestant Faith we have well over twenty five thousand different sects, just like we have over twenty five thousand "townships" in the United States. Just imagine what would happen to our legal system if each Township interpreted the Constitution as *they* say fit. There would be utter chaos within our legal system.

When I have asked most Protestant how one goes about seeking interpretation of Holy Scripture, the usual answer is that they pray to the "Holy Spirit" for guidance.

How is it then that the "Holy Spirit" will give an Anglican one answer, and an Episcopalian another contradictory answer? i.e. Homosexuality! Does this not seem rather ludicrous? There is no Central Authority among the Protestants regarding interpretation of Holy Scripture and as a result there are many, many different interpretations of the same Biblical passage.

Some will say that "Faith" alone is enough for Salvation. Another will say, "Good Works" are the criteria for Salvation. Another Faith will say that we are ALL going to heaven, as there is no Hell. Then another will say that God is All forgiving so we will see Paradise. Still, several other will say there are a select few who are predestined to go to Heaven, and others who do not subscribe to this theology.

Most Protestants Faiths believe that Jesus had earthly sibling through his mother Mary. Others do not accept this belief.

Most Protestant Faiths reject the Perpetual Virginity of Mary, while some others do believe in the Perpetual Virginity, and also Her bodily Assumption into Heaven. The Anglican/Episcopal Faith celebrates the Nativity of Mary on September 8th each year, as does the Catholic Church.

On May 16th, 2005, the Anglican Church issued a joint statement with the Catholic Church regarding Marianalogy. The Statement known as the "Seattle Statement" was signed by Catholic Archbishop Alexander Brunett and Anglican Archbishop Peter Camley. The Statement was an agreement within the two Faiths as to the **Perpetual Virginity of Mary, and Her bodily Assumption into Heaven,** and that this is "being consonant" with Holy Scripture.

Now here you have one of the Founding Faiths of the Reformation agreeing with Catholicism, while others of the "Johnny come latelys" disagree.

Many believe that an infant should not be baptized, while others take a contrary view. Most do not look upon the rite of marriage as a Sacrament, while some do. Then there is the matter of divorce. Most Protestant Faiths believe in divorce, while some do not.

How can twenty five thousand different Protestant Faiths come up with twenty five thousand different interpretations of Scripture and then have the audacity to say they are <u>guided by the "Holy Spirit"</u>?

Look at the Constitution of the United States. The Constitution is to the United States, what the Bible is to Christianity; it is the Law of the Land. Imagine if you will, if each States interpreted the Constitution as *they* saw fit. Imagine then, if each county within the State took a different interpretation of the Law, and administered it as *they* saw fit. Add to this dilemma, if then each Township took a contrary view of the Law, and administered it as *they* saw fit. Our Legal system would be, as is the Protestant Movement, in shambles.

What chaos there would be, regarding enforcing the Law? So it is within the Protestant community. There are over twenty five thousand different interpretations of the "Law". There are even some Faiths, Lutheran and Anglican/Episcopalian, who differ internally. As a result of these differences in Scriptural interpretation, the Anglican/Episcopalian Community is on the verge of still another schism.

I had asked one couple, from a Nondenominational Church, with whom I had a religious discussion, what was the source of their interpretation of Scripture. They replied that they do not take interpretation from man but from God. They must be very special people to have God Interpret Scripture for them.

In the Parable of the "Sower of the Seeds", Jesus was asked by the Apostles, why He spoke in Parables. Jesus asked them if they knew what the message was, and they replied that they did. Did not Jesus then say to the Apostles, "To YOU is given to know the Mysteries of Heaven, but to Them it is NOT given. For hearing they do not hear, and seeing they do not see. Blessed are YOUR eyes, for They see, and Your ears Hear". This was not a Power given to the multitude, but to His Church.

Indubitably there are very many Protestants who believe in their "heart" that they are on the Right Path to Salvation. How does one explain the differences in Scriptural passages between different Faiths? The Anglicans believe in the Perpetual Virginity of Mary, and Her bodily Assumption into Heaven, while other Protestant Faiths believe any homage to Mary is contrary to Christianity.

Some Faiths accept homosexuality; others decry homosexuality as an abomination (sin). Not only do some of the Faiths accept Homosexuality, but have gone so far as to ordain them as priests/ministers and also install some as Bishops.

Now we even have several prominent Protestant ministers stating that Jesus was a homosexual. This is HERESY, and Protestantism does nothing to combat this blatant assault on the Sanctity and Divinity of Jesus.

Some Faiths will except one area of contention, and deny another, while several others will believe just the opposite.

Is this not what Jesus prophesied?

**"Seeing they do not see
Hearing they do not hear".**

Did not Jesus give this Power to <u>His church</u>?
What I have personally experienced, in my discussions with Protestants, is their ability to quote chapter and verse of Scripture to defend their belief. Invariably they will quote the Old Testament. My answer to them generally was:

"What did Jesus Say?"

Are we not Christians and as such a Follower of Christ?
On one occasion, while discussing the Forgiveness of Sins, with a Protestant, he denied the authority of the Catholic priests to forgive sins. He explained that one has only to pray to God for forgiveness.

When I pointed out to him what Jesus had said to Peter, quoting the Passage in Scripture that said:

**"I give to you the Key to the Kingdom of Heaven.
Whose Sins you shall forgive they are forgiven.
Whose sins you shall retain, they are retained".**

The response from the young man denied the Sacrament of Reconciliation, saying that the Power was given to Peter alone and not the Church. To accept that belief, is to believe that Jesus come down to Earth, experienced a human childhood, plus His ministry, His Passion and Crucifixion and Ascension, and limited this Power to Peter alone. How ludicrous that is.

When all else fails, the usual rhetoric is Anti-Catholicism, plus the myth that Peter was never in Rome. It is my finding that serious Protestant scholars no longer deny that Peter was in Rome and Crucified in Rome, and is buried in the Vatican along side the body of St Paul.

Previous to his martyrdom, Peter Baptized converts in the Tiber River (Eusebeus Hist. Eccl.), and Irenaeus. Peter wrote his first epistle about 63 A.D from Rome. Peter noted that he was writing from Babylon, which is an historical reference to Rome. This happened just before the Neroian Persecutions in which both Peter and Paul were crucified. Peter chose to be crucified upside down, believing he was not worthy to suffer the same fate as did Jesus.

History records that the Christians hastened to remove the body of Peter before the Romans could have it destroyed. In their haste, it was necessary to cut off Peter's feet and hurriedly buried it were the Vatican now stands. Pope Paul VI, in late 1960's commissioned an excavation underneath the Vatican to see if the body of Peter could be found. A body, the size of Peter minus his feet was indeed found, and certified as that of the Patron Saint of the Catholic Church.

Regarding the sanctity of marriage, I was given a lot of mumbo jumbo regarding the conditions under which a divorce is granted, and remarriage approved. One has but to look at the multitude of people, who profess a belief in Jesus and His Word, yet enter into marriage after marriage, after numerous marriages.

What did Jesus say?

When Jesus was told by the elders, that Moses had given them a Bill of Divorce, and did Jesus agree with that. Jesus replied that indeed Moses had given them a Bill of Divorce because of the hard heartedness of the Israelites. Further, Jesus said, that:

> "From the beginning of time, God create Man and Woman
> and the two shall leave Father and Mother
> and cleave only unto each other.
> What God has joined together, let no Man put asunder".

Jesus added further, that for a man to divorce his wife and to marry another, that man has committed adultery. Also for another to marry a divorced person, they have committed adultery.

With the election of Cardinal Ratzinger as Pope Benedict XVI, the 266th consecutive Pope of the Roman catholic Church, many Protestants bewailed the fact that Pope Benedict was a conservative and would adhere to the Catholic teachings on Marriage, Homosexuality, Divorce, and the Sacraments. They proclaimed that the Catholic Church was out of line with the 21st Century, and if is to survive it must adapt to the morals of the present day. They said the Catholic church was living in the past.

The question I would ask the nay Sayers is:

"Does the Teachings of the Church adapt to Society, or does Society Conform to the Teachings of the Church."

Today there are twenty five thousand "Christian Sects", each teaching their own theology as to the Word of God. To me these sects have two things in common.

- The King James Bible
- Anti-Catholicism

A great many Protestants of various denominations with whom I have had occasion to "discuss" religion, all have used the King James Bible as their reference. When I asked the question as to "how is it that so many different Faiths, all using the same Book, have arrived at a contrary interpretation as to what your particular Faith is Teaching", they have never been able to give me an intelligent answer.

When I push further for an explanation, of the source of their interpretation of Scripture they usually reply that they Pray to the Holy Spirit for guidance. I would then ask:

"If the Episcopalian and the Baptist both Pray to the Holy Spirit, why is it that they both come up with a contrary answer? Then, what of the Methodist and the Seventh Day Adventist? Is not their Theology contrary to each other? What of the Lutheran and the Presbyterian Faiths. Are they not in conflict with each others teachings?

Many individuals, would state that it "really did not matter which Christian church" you attended. To me, to admit that another Church could <u>possibly be the True Church is to admit that your church could be the wrong Church</u>.

In my discourse with Protestants, their response invariably has been anti Catholic rhetoric. Whether it was the Harvest Bible Church, the Church in the Word or several Lutheran Churches, all invited me to come and to hear their sermons. My reply has been and still is, "I don't want to hear sermons, and **I want to discuss your theology."** None of these Pastors have had the time to discuss theology with me. I could come and listen, but they did not have the time to answer my questions regarding their teachings. All, to me, have an anti Catholic agenda.

In the case of the Harvest Bible Church, they deny being anti Catholic, yet their hand book is filled with anti Catholic rhetoric. Yet there is not one word about the Anglican Faith which teaches a theology contrary to theirs. Then again, what of the Lutherans, the United Church of Christ and the United Methodists? Each of these denominations has a vastly different theology of that taught by Harvest Bible.

Harvest Bible is not unique in their presentation of their Scriptural beliefs. There are twenty five thousand Faiths and twenty five thousand different interpretations of Scripture.

It is my understanding that there are two accepted Sacraments in most protestant Faiths. The first Sacrament being Baptism, the other Holy Eucharist. Within the Catholic Church there are seven Sacraments.

1. Baptism
2. Reconciliation
3. Holy Eucharist
4. Confirmation
5. Matrimony
6. Holy Orders
7. Anointing of the Sick

I have often wondered why those of the Protestant persuasion only accept two Sacraments. The Sacrament of Baptism and Holy Eucharist, I can readily understand, but not accepting the other five is beyond my understanding.

The first, Holy Eucharist, we agree was instituted by Jesus at the Last Supper, when He directed the Apostles to do Likewise. With Baptism, Jesus instituted the Sacrament by submitting to the ritual of Baptism through John the Baptist, and the Holy Spirit descended upon Him and proclaimed "This is My Beloved Son in whom I am well pleased".

However most Protestant Faiths do not baptize infants and some do not recognize Baptism as a Sacrament. It is my belief that a prerequisite for Salvation was Baptism. Our Lord had said "that to enter the Kingdom of Heaven, one MUST be Baptized. " Unless you are Baptized, you would not gain Salvation" Here again we have several different Protestant Faiths that do not believe in Baptism, yet NO Protestant Faith will denounce them as false teachers. They can ONLY find fault with Catholicism.

No one has been able to tell me the fate of young babies who have not been baptized. At age eight days, Jesus was taken to the Temple to be Blessed. How many young Protestant children who have suffered an early death are being denied the "Kingdom of Heaven" because they have not been baptized?

Every Protestant, with whom I have had religious discussions, claims they are preaching the Word of God, and living the Word of God. They maybe too a degree, but as a noted radio commentator often has said:

What is the rest of the story?

Reconciliation

Most Protestants do not look upon Reconciliation as a Sacrament. What was it the Jesus said to the Apostles?

"I give to you the Keys to the Kingdom of Heaven. Whose Sins YOU shall Forgive, they are Forgiven. Whose Sins YOU shall retain, they are Retained."

Is this not a directive directly from Our Lord? What could be plainer? Most every Protestant, with whom I have had discourse regarding this Sacrament, has come up with basically the same response. They believe that in "just" asking God for forgiveness, forgiveness will be granted.

One individual stated that he believed that the "Power" to forgive Sins was given to Peter alone. However this very same individual denied the Supremacy of Peter. This is just a bit confusing. One hand Peter has Power to forgive Sins, but on the other hand he is just another individual with NO power. This is just the sort of contradictions that I find when I am able to have a protracted discourse with a Protestant.

It is known in psychiatry and in social work, that to over come ones failings (sins), it is always best to meet with an arbiter and admit ones faults. This is the mode followed by AA and like organizations. When we unburden ourselves with a "friend", the friend tends to take a sympathetic view in favor of the friend.

Mostly, the friend will try to pacify us and not get to the root of the problem.

Prayer is a powerful tool, especially when combined with the Sacrament of Reconciliation and repentance. It is a help to admit to oneself that they had done a serious wrong, but we must confess and ATONE for the wrong (sin).

As a Catholic, we pray before confessing to a priest,

> "Come Holy Ghost;
> Help me to know my Sins,
> Be heartily sorry for them
> And repent them sincerely.

In the past, most priests would require a litany of various prayers as part of the penance. Today, more often the penance could be to do acts of charity. How easy it is for us to say to ourselves, "I am sorry". It is MUCH more difficult to say to another "I am sorry". Saying "I am sorry" does not rectify the problem. If we broke a favorite item of anyone, to say I am sorry is a start, but it would be expected that we find the means to correct the error. **Confession and repentance**.

HOLY ORDERS

Almost all Protestant Faiths do **NOT** look upon the Ordination of a Minister as a Sacrament. Many future Protestant Ministers will attend some Theological College and get a degree in Divinity. However MANY Protestant Ministers acquire a "degree" in Divinity from schools of ill repute. Some will attain a degree from an "on line" Church. On December 24th, 2005 I was "ordained" by a Protestant International Church in Tennessee. All that was required of me was a few dollars to print up the certificate. For a few dollars more I was given a Doctorate in Divinity. This was followed by acquiring a PHD in Theology. With the certificates granted me, I can legally officiate as a minister at a Protestant wedding, anywhere in the USA, and for that matter, anywhere in the world.

To push the "envelope" further, I inquired about receiving the rank of Bishop, which was offered to me for a mere $25.00, to print the certificate. The internet is replete with these opportunities to become a Protestant minister.

- No schooling
- No examination
- No accountability
- Tax free income

My own research has uncovered many individual who proclaim themselves as a Minister of God, and yet cannot show where they have had any formal accepted religious training. There are several who are undocumented immigrants, and some who are "former" drug addicts and also numerous pedophiles and sex offenders. We will get into this aspect later.

What I find most interesting and beguiling, is that one faction of Protestantism, is a Faith that names itself after a Founder of the Reformation, and has itself been divided as to Theology, while all the time teaching a Theology contrary to it's founder.

Seemingly, all Protestant Faiths have in one form or another deviated from the Theology of its Founder. It appears that anyone can call themselves a Protestant Minister, and establish a Religion. To become a Protestant Minister, one does not need a formal education, just a certificate from an "on line" Church, or even in some instances, just the ability to print a certificate of ordination.

Of the twenty five thousand Protestant Faiths, I would bet that just a very small handful of the ministers have had a formal religious education from a "mainline" institute of Theology. Yet these so called ministers have as much legal standing in the Protestant Faiths, as another who has been enrolled in a Religious school of higher learning, and has had an examination before recognized instructors, and has been tested and certified as a minister.

Anyone can become a Protestant minister, no formal education, no tests, no accountability, and preach *their own brand of Theology*. There is no authority within the Protestant community to govern or authenticate any of these "so called" ministers.

For years I have heard the Protestant community wail against the Catholic Church, accusing the Catholic as Idolaters, and Marianoligists, because of the veneration of the Mother of Jesus. Yet, these same Protestant will remain mute when one of their members Faiths labels Jesus as a homosexual. What heresy! What a sacrilege!

What I find most disturbing is that while very many Protestants will accept unqualified, untested, self-interested individual as Ministers for their beliefs in the Word of God, yet these very same individuals would not hesitate to seek the removal of a teacher in the public school system that has no credentials and no certification, regarding education.

I can see why the Protestant Faiths are adverse to a standard education and training for their Ministry. With Protestantism, the main goal is to bring about the destruction of the Catholic Church. If Mainline Protestant Faiths were living up to the Theology of the Founders of the Reformation, they would act as the Founders did, and expose the charlatans and frauds that have invaded the Protestant movement.

CONFIRMATION

Almost all Protestants will claim that their Faith is derived from Scripture. They have stated to me, that if it is not in Scripture, they cannot follow it. If it is in Scripture, then they will follow it. Protestants do not accept Confirmation as a Sacrament, because they cannot find Biblical reference to the Act.

As Our good Lord has said,

"They have eyes to see, and do not see, and ears to hear and do not hear."

Of the nay Sayers, I would ask, "what was twelve year old Jesus accomplishing, by being brought to Jerusalem? Was it not to be confirmed it the Faith? Are not all Jewish boys "confirmed" into their Faith at about age twelve?

Confirmation is just another step in being versed in your Faith. To be confirmed, one must know his/her religion and have completed good works.

<u>Faith with Good Works is essential for Salvation</u>. There cannot be Faith without Good Works. There can be good works without faith. Did not our Lord say that even the pagans do good works? Good works does not constitute faith

ANOINTING of the SICK

Here again we have a difference with our Protestant brethren. They completely disregard the importance and significance of the Sacrament. What could be more logical then a Sacrament to "usher" us into the Kingdom of Heaven? Do we not prepare the body for internment? What could more logical than to prepare the Soul for our journey to Heaven? In Baptism we have a Sacrament at our life's beginning, and at death we have Extreme Unction (Anointing of the Sick) to cleanse our Soul for the passage to Heaven.

MARRIAGE – DIVORCE

Here is, in my belief the greatest failing of the Protestant Faiths. Most of them do not recognize the Rite of Marriage as a Sacrament. I have often asked myself, Why? No one member of a Protestant persuasion has been able to give me an intelligent answer. What most have said is that it is not mentioned in Scripture.

Considering that the Protestants use the same Bible, and there are twenty five thousand different sects, EACH having a different interpretation of Scripture, it is no wonder that they cannot *"see the forest for the trees"*.

Did not Our Lord begin His Ministry by performing His First (of many) miracle, at the marriage feast at Cana? Our Lord turned water into wine. Several Protestant Faiths prohibit the partaking of wine and of dancing, yet here we have Our Lord attending a marriage and in a sense providing the wine. I, for one, do know of any Jewish wedding that is devoid of dancing.

Here again, we have a paradox. The Protestants say that marriage is not a Sacrament, just a ritual. What was it our Lord said regarding marriage, and what do most Protestant ministers say at the conclusion of the wedding ceremony?

WHAT <u>GOD</u> HAS JOINED TOGETHER, LET NO MAN PUT ASSUNDER.

Is this not a Command from Our Lord? Is not the Commands of Our Lord a Sacrament? What is Holy Matrimony if not a Sacrament?

To take this a step further, which results in diluting of the importance of marriage, the Protestant find many reason for justifying divorce.

One young couple with whom I had spent several hours discussing religion constantly came up with reasons to justify divorce. Invariably they came up with a passage from the Old Testament, or passages from the New Testament, taken out of context.

What was it Jesus said regarding divorce, when the Pharases told Him that Moses granted them a Bill of Divorce? Did not Our Lord reply, that Moses granted them a "Bill of Divorce" because they (the Jews) were hard hearted? What was Our Lords reply?

From the beginning of time, God created both Man and Woman.
That they should leave both father and mother,
And the two shall become one
And cleave <u>ONLY</u> unto each other.

What GOD has Joined together, let NO man put asunder.

FURTHER Our Lord added

"For a man to divorce his wife and marry another, he has committed adultery. And for another person to marry a divorced person, they have committed adultery."

What could be clearer in defining a Sacrament, than the Command of God?

I have heard, many times, a Protestant minister, while officiating at a marriage use the admonition, "we are here, in the PRESENCE of God, and closing with the phrase, "what God has Joined together". Etc, etc. What could be clearer then that, that in here we have a command from God?

Then we have very many Protestant couples, engaging in divorce after divorce after divorce, and still Protestant ministers will perform these unholy rituals. Homes are torn apart, children are shuffled between parents.

Invariably, the divorced spouse will remarry someone who is a clone of their former spouse. In very many cases, a man will leave his wife and children for a MUCH younger woman and the Protestant minister will perform the wedding. Most of the time, the couple will opt for a civil ceremony, which is recognized by their adopted Protestant sect.

The Catholic Church does not recognize, as a valid marriage, one that is preformed without the sanction of the Church.

Many Protestants will claim that marriage is now passé. They point to the high rate of divorce, citing that fully half the marriages fail. In and of itself this is true. But what is:

The rest of the Story

When marriages are an integral part of a religious ceremony, the rate of divorce is about two in ten. Faith, Religion, and Commitment are an integral part of any successful marriage.

The youth today want to "try it before they buy it". As a

result, very many couples base their desire for marriage on "how good he/she is in bed. Marriage today is based on sex, not on a desire for home and family. The desire for sex goes out the window when she has to clean his dirty and stained underwear, and he has to put up with her "periods". The young female at work or the "hunk" at the exercise class are very inviting sexual objects.

To recite the very many pitfalls to a marriage based on sex, would entail writing another book. A marriage based on Love, and a STRONG belief in God and His Commands, will for the most part result in a successful marriage.

Many Protestants will say that we Catholics are hypocrites, in that we allow divorce, but we call it an annulment. What is an annulment compared to a divorce?

In a divorce, recognized by most Protestant Faiths, each of the couple decides that they are incompatible and seek a separation. Some will "accuse" the other of infidelity, which in many cases will be true of *both* parties. Yet a Protestant minister will officiate at the second, third and even the fourth or more ceremonies. For a Protestant minister to intone the admonition "What God has Joined together, let no man put asunder" time after time to the same individual, is hypocrisy.

Now we come to an annulment. An annulment is granted if either party to the marriage, entered into the marriage under false pretenses. Following are some of the grounds for an annulment.

Either party being coerced into the marriage
Either party lied regarding the rising of children
Either party did not disclose a physical or drug problem
Either party lied about wanting children
Either party did not disclose a past relationship that resulted in an offspring
Either party used the marriage to gain legal status

There are other reasons for an annulment, and under some circumstances some of the above may not apply. For every annulment, there are a thousand or more divorces. A Catholic may seek and receive a civil divorce, but they may not marry another and remain a Catholic and receive the Sacraments. In the eyes of the Catholic Church, to marry another person, after a divorce, will preclude receiving the Sacraments, including Holy Communion.

Holy Eucharist

While most Protestant Faiths regard Holy Eucharist as a Sacrament, there are several who do not. Among them are the Baptists who regard the Holy Communion as a memorial service, which may be offered once a month.

Also, most Protestants deride the Catholics for their belief in Transubstantiation. They find it difficult to accept that the bread is in reality the Body and the wine the Blood of Christ. To me, the Host, without Transubstantiation is just a ritual, not a Sacrament. With Transubstantiation the Holy Eucharist is a Sacrament.

At the Last Supper, Our Lord took the bread and broke it and said, "This is my Body". Then taking the wine he said,"This is My Blood "He then commanded us to go and do likewise. Earlier in His Ministry, Our Lord had said "Unless you eat my Body and Drink My Blood" you cannot gain Heaven. When He had said this, many of his followers left Him, as they could not understand what He meant. Just like the Protestants seemingly cannot understand the Word of God.

For many, various acts and deeds in Scripture are difficult to fathom. Such as:

The Virgin Birth
The Star of Bethlehem
The three Magi
Turning water into wine
Turning five loaves and two fishes into a meal for thousands
Raising the dead
The Resurrection
The Ascension
The Holy Spirit

Transubstantiation
Father-Son-Holy Spirit in One Person

What we have among our Protestant brethren is a "pick and choose" approach to Scripture. Sort of what we experience when we go to a cafeteria. We take a little of this and a little of that and ignore what is, to us, not palatable.

Today many nondenominational Faiths are gaining some members by offering them a belief that is palatable with today's society's morals. Mainline Faiths are losing members, and are, in some instances facing a schism.

Episcopalian, Lutheran and Methodist are undergoing internal strife regarding the acceptance of homosexuality. Baptists have had a former United States President leave one faction of the Baptist convention, and join another as he proclaimed that the Baptist were behind modern times.

With regard to Transubstantiation, I personally do not understand it, but I do accept it. It is part of my Faith. I have been asked many times, "how can you accept something that you do not understand?

I do not understand gravity. I do not understand, that if Earth is spinning at the rate of 1,000 miles per hour, how is it that when I jump in the air, I still come down in the same place I jumped off from. I do not understand how all the water that we call rain is up in the clouds, and we can fly through the clouds and not get wet.

The theory of relativity is beyond my comprehension, but I realize that it is an accepted fact. These are but a few of our earthly puzzles, that we all accept, and yet they are minuscule when compared with God's miracles. Too pick and choose the miracle of God, is to me, to deny the Omnipotence of Our Creator.

Baptism

Here we have a Sacrament that almost all Protestants agree, as being necessary in order to gain Heaven. However they do disagree amongst themselves as to when the Sacrament should be administered. Most of the Protestant Faiths admonish the Catholic Church for Baptizing infants. They state that the one being baptized must be an adult, or at least an individual who is of the age of "consent".

Here we have a dilemma. What happens to the child that is not baptized and then dies? There is quite a bit of infant mortality. Does not Scripture say that to gain Heaven, one MUST be baptized?

What most Protestants bring up is that they can find no justification in Scripture for baptizing infants. What was it Our Lord had said regarding small children?

**"Do not hinder them from coming to me
For such is the Kingdom of Heaven"**

Here again we have the Protestants caught in a dilemma. How can infants gain Heaven if they are not Baptized? Children, in the eyes of Our Lord are very special.

In the United States, as it is in most countries, when adults are admitted to citizenship, their minor offspring are also enrolled as citizens of the Nation. The child, upon reaching maturity can, if they so desire, renounce that citizenship. So it is with our children. They are born into the Faith of their parents. It is a parent's responsibility to educate the child in their Faith.

9

One fold-One Shepherd

Out Lord had warned us that there are other Sheep (people) that are not of His Fold, but there Shall Be One Fold and ONE Shepherd.

Today there are well over twenty five thousand Protestant sects that "claim" they are followers of Our Lord, but their theology is vastly different from the Word of God. Let us look at some of the excuses that are promoted by a vast majority of Protestant sects, in denying the tenets of the Catholic Faith.

Over the years I have heard many, many complaints regarding the Catholic church. Some complaints (excuses) are valid, and some are just plain excuses by someone who in reality cannot justify their leaving or not joining the Church.

Some have expressed the opinion that they left the Church because they did not like a priest, or the real or imagined actions of a priest. This is comparable to some of the idiot Hollywood movie stars who threatened to leave the United States if Bush (42) was reelected President in 2004. He was, but none of them did.

I personally had a lack of respect for a former Pastor at St Francis De Sales Catholic Church in Lake Zurich, Illinois. While I respected him as a priest, I could not respect him as a leader of the parish. As a result I and my family did leave the parish. *Not the Church.* We joined another Catholic parish. When the former pastor was reassigned, we did return to our parish in

Lake Zurich. In my humble opinion, he was a dedicated priest, but a very poor leader.

None of us in life will have everything the way we want them to be or believe how it should be. Just imagine the chaos there would be, if we left our cities, States, or Country, every time we did not agree with our leaders.

Former President Clinton, in my opinion was a sleaze ball, but he was the leader of our Country. The Foundation of our Country is the Constitution. That is the Law of the Land. That is what we base our beliefs on, just as our Faith is based on the Word of God. Priests come and go, but the Word of God remains. This is what we base our Faith on, not the man preaching.

One man I met joined the Catholic Church because of the Heroic actions of a priest in time of conflict. The priest risked his life to administer the Last Rites to a dying soldier .The priest is a man, capable of doing good and evil. I told my friend that the reason he should join the Catholic Church is due to its unaltered Theology from the time of Christ, even into today, whereas the Protestant faiths are in a continual state of flux. What they taught yesterday, is changed today, in an effort to accommodate their flock.

Another left the Church because of the accusation against Catholic priests. In most cases the accusations were legitimate. What is not very well publicized is the fact that for every Catholic priest that was accused of sexual impropriety, there are over two Protestant ministers who have perpetrated the same heinous crimes.

The monstrous acts by both Catholic priests and Protestant ministers are blight on the Christian movement. All of these individual should be severely punished, and they should be forbidden to have contact with any minor children. Whether it is a Catholic priest or a Protestant minister, their abominable actions are no reason for leaving a Faith. May I be so bold as to remind you that Our Lord had admonished His Apostles as "The Spirit is Willing, but the Flesh is Weak". There are good and bad in every Faith, and a Faith should be judge on What is the True Word of God.

There are those who have left the Church because of the actions of another member of the congregation. That may be a reason for leaving a parish, as I had, but not a reason for leaving the Church.

There are some who have said that they left the Church because the Masses are too crowded. What, may I ask, has this to do with Scripture? To me, it is like someone leaving New York City, because it is too crowded and moving to Canada.

There is a vast difference between an excuse and a reason. A young man I had working for me many years ago, would come into work late many times. I would ask him "why are you late"? His reply would be either that the traffic was heavy or his mother did not waken him in time. That was his excuse. The real *reason* was that he did not start out on time, and allow for a traffic problem. As to his other excuse, regarding his mother not waking him on time, only showed that he was not mature enough to take responsibilities for his own well being.

An excuse if an effort to put blame on something we believe we cannot control. Leaving home late was within his control, which he did not exercise, along with taking his own responsibility for the alarm clock.

Many of those with whom I have spoken regarding leaving the church, or not joining the Church have given me many "excuses" but no one has given me a valid "reason".

Another excuse for leaving the Church was the dull sermons given by the priest. Some people do not hear what is being said. Others are in rapture by a dynamic speaker. Then there are those who look to be "entertained".

We have but to look at the "new" approach to teaching the Faith. There was Jim and Tammy Faye, Jim Jones, and Adolph Hitler. All of them were leaders who mesmerized their followers, and finally led them to destruction.

It is not how it is said, but what is said that makes the difference between fact and fancy. In November 1863 Edward Evert the celebrated orator of his day, gave a two hour dynamic speech at the dedication of the cemetery at Gettysburg. No one remembers what this noted orator said that day, but at the time, he was wildly acclaimed.

Abraham Lincoln was not an orator. He gave what at the time was considered a dull two minute speech. A speech that today is considered a classic in that it had a message that lives on today.

In seeking God, most people see what they want to see and hear what they want to hear. Is this not what Our Lord warned us about? Did not Our Lord warn us that many would come and preach in His name, but that would only lead to destruction.

As a result of hearing what one wants to hear and seeing what one wants to see has resulted in well over twenty five thousand vastly different Christian theologies. How can there be One Fold and One Shepherd, when there are so very many different orders being given.

They were there when I needed someone

Here again is another excuse for leaving the Church, or joining another faith. Did not Our Lord tell us the even the unbelievers would do good works. I personally know of some individual who have left their Catholic Faith and joined a nondenominational Faith, because, in their hour of need, someone was there to aid and assist them. That in and of itself, is an admirable act. But it does not justify joining a Faith, that very well could be expounding a religious tenet contrary to that of Our Savior.

When it comes to charitable works, no religious organization can come anywhere near the works of the Catholic Church and it various organizations. Here in the Chicago land area, Catholic Charities provides hundreds of thousand of meals to those in needs, <u>regardless of their religious affiliation</u>. This does not include the works of individual parishes which provide hot meals on a regular basis, again to those in need, not asking the recipients as to what, if any church they are a member of.

The food banks, operated by the various parishes, provide good wholesome food staples that are donated <u>by the parishioners themselves, not a collection of surplus, going out of date foods that are dispensed by several grocery chains</u>. The food dispensed by the food bank is food bought and paid for by individuals within the parish.

As one who has been active in the St Vincent De Paul Society, I know first hand of many, many instances of charitable works preformed by the Society. These acts of Good Works are in themselves separate from the Works of Catholic Charities. With both the food banks and the works of St Vincent De Paul, aid is given freely to anyone who is in need. In many instances the organization will be informed by the police or a member of the township government, that there is an individual or family that is in need, and does not qualify for government assistance. The Church and its various organizations are there to render assistance.

I personally have been scammed by an individual claiming that they were in dire need of assistance. The assistance was given, no questions ask, only to find out later that this individual would go from parish to parish and perpetrate the same scam. No mater how many cases any organization would process, there will always be some who "fall through the cracks" and are missed.

A very good example of charitable giving is the tsunami relief efforts in 2004-2005. Here we have Catholics donating funds and goods to aid mostly Moslems. The amount of money Catholics raised for the relief and assistance exceeded their own goal by tens of millions of dollars, and they exceeded their goal by 50%. Their agencies raised more than $200 million. This was more than what was donated by numerous relief agencies put together. Following is a partial list.

UNICEF
CARE USA
Lutheran World Relief
Salvation Army

American Jewish World Relief
Church World Services
United Methodists

Catholic Relief Service has a budget of $500 million dollars, and dispenses aid in over 99 foreign countries. Moslem or Jew, Catholic or Protestant, Hindu or Atheist, it makes no difference. Where there is a need, the CRS are there. This relief effort is not used to proselytize but only to do God's work. He did tell us to do good to those who would harm us. Even with all these good works, there are many, very many who are in need, and still "fall through the cracks".

The Catholic Church has founded and administered more hospitals, orphanages, and social services than all other Faiths combined.

Another service by the Catholic Church is with young boy and girls doing good works to those in need. Many local parishes will send a number of the youth, with adult chaperone to depressed area, and to do acts of charity. Painting, cleaning, cutting grass, baby sitting, etc, etc, etc, are just some of the projects. The youths do a multitude of Works of Faith. Their one goal is to aid those who are in need, not to proselytize.

There are good and bad people in every faith. We should not join a Faith because of the deeds of a person, or leave a Faith for the same reason, but only because of the "Word of God".

10

Past Wrongs of the Catholic Church And The Reformation

If I heard it once time, I heard it a hundred times about the "sins" of the Catholic Church 500 years ago.
(Not the sex scandal of today's times we will deal with that a little later in detail).
They will rail about some Pope and what they "heard" what he did or did not do. They point out the "Spanish" Inquisition, the burning of heretics and the torture of enemies of the Church.

While many rail about some Pope of several hundreds of years ago, not too many make mention of the Popes of today. Pope John Paul II is a very good example Here we have a man who lived through Nazi occupation, followed by Soviet occupation. It is widely accepted that Pope John Paul was instrumental in bringing about the downfall of International Communism.

When Pope John Paul II said Mass in Grant Park, there were by several account anywhere from a half million to seven Hundred thousands souls at the Mass, I included. What I found most edifying was that with this vast multitude of people, one could hear the birds sing. It seemed that everyone was enraptured by the man. He was Holiness personified.

When he "passed" on there was the greatest congregation of Heads of State the World had ever seen. Never in history had so many Kings, Queens, Presidents, Prime Ministers of almost every Nation assembled for this occasion. This was truly a tribute to the greatness of the Holy man. Most every Religion in the World also honored John Paul II.

While the Vatican has a representative at the United Nations, a great many Nations, including the United States have sent Ambassadors to the Vatican. No other Faith in the World can claim this Honor.

What everyone does, is to equate what happened 500 years ago with what is happening today. What were the times like then? Many a Nobel would love to have the connivances that many of our families, that are today <u>living in poverty</u>.

o   There was no central heat
There was no air conditioning
There were no frozen foods
There was very little fresh fruit and meats
Only a select few had an education
Very few could read or write
There were very few books
Women were chattel

With the advent of the Protestant Reformation, the Western World was faced with three major religious beliefs coming into conflict with each other. As a result ALL three of them employed tactics, that today we would consider barbaric

But, that was then, and now is now!

Heretics and those who were thought to have spread heresies, were either executed or suffered severe torture. Yes even the Catholics did it, along with the Protestants and the Moslems. Even the Anglican Church, under Henry VIII was born of blood and torture, beheading and burning, along with confiscation of properties.

For every act that one Pope or another has been accused of, Luther, Calvin, Zwingali and others acted in the same vain. It was a time that religion was in a battle for its existence. While Protestantism threatened the Catholic Church, the greatest enemy of Christianity was then, as it is today, *Islam*.

Moslems had conquered the lands of Eastern Europe, North Africa, and had occupied half of the Iberian Peninsula. When the Moslems conquered a land, the populations either converted to Islam, or were eliminated.

While I can find no note in history of Luther sending a heretic to the "stake", he was (in my humble opinion) responsible for not only the death of thousands of Christians, but also the loss of thousands of Christians to Islam.

In the 1520's, while Suleiman was marching on Hungary the Nobles of Hungary appealed to the German Nobility to send aid. Luther exhorted the German Nobles to ignore the appeal, as he declared that Suleiman was the "Wrath of God", sent to punish the Catholics, and it was far better to be ruled by a wise Moslem, (Suleiman), than to be ruled by a stupid Christian (the Pope).

On August 29th, 1526, at the battle of Mohacs the entire Hungarian army, Monarchy and Nobility was destroyed in a matter of only two hours. It was a slaughter of the greatest magnitude. King Louis and Arch Bishop Tomori were among the victims. Well over *two thousand prisoners were **beheaded the following day***. This in turn opened the road to the gates of Vienna, and in turn Northern Europe.

The attack on Vienna aroused the German Nobility. Luther himself publicly prayed for deliverance from the "terror of Islam". Luther then suspended his tirades against the Pope and wrote his:

De Bello Trucia

Luther then acknowledged that Suleiman, not the Pope was the true enemy of God. However by that time, Suleiman and his army had occupied a great portion of the Balkans. Where Suleiman went, Islam followed, so as a result of the hesitancy of the German aid to Hungary, tens of thousands of Souls were lost to Christianity, and Islam had taken root in Southeast Europe.

Almost all Protestants are unaware of this episode in the "birth" of the Reformation. It appears that all Faiths were "born in blood". Did not Our Lord predict what would happen?

Did not Our Lord predict that because of His Teachings, that brother would fight brother, father against son, mother against daughter, friend and neighbor against each other etc, etc, etc?

I wonder how many Protestants are cognizant of what happened within the first 20 to 30 years of the Reformation. Calvin and others accused Luther as being too Catholic in his theology. This could very well be the foundation of the Anti-Catholic rhetoric that persists today.

With the death of Luther, John Calvin appealed to Phillip Melanchthon, Luther's successor, for both Faiths to come to a Central Belief. There were differences in what both Calvin and Luther had been teaching, and Calvin said that is was **IMPARATIVE** that they (the Protestants) come to a Central Theology. Calvin warned that unless there was a <u>Single interpretation of Scripture</u>, the whole future of the Reformation would be placed in jeopardy. Failure to unify would in turn spawn other diverse and diluting theologies, which in turn would bring into question the basis of the Reformation.

Now let's look at what has happened as a result of the failure of the Founding Fathers of the Reformation to Unify. Five hundred years after Luther started the Reformation, the Protestant has been deluged with over twenty five thousand diverse Protestant sects, each one having its own interpretation of Scripture. Many Protestant have advised me that it really did not matter which (Protestant) faith you adopted, just so you follow the Laws of God. They will say that with a "straight face", and then will almost always end their dissertation with a tirade against the Pope and the Catholic Church.

Follow God's Law! Is Luther right and Calvin wrong? They both had a distinct difference in their theology. Then, if you are saying that Calvin is wrong, then is Wesley right? What then of Zwingali? We have John Smyth who disagrees with both Calvin and Luther. Along comes William Nettle who in turn disagrees with his predecessors. John Aston not only disagreed with Luther and Calvin, but also denied the protocol of Three Persons in One God. Charles Russell then comes into the picture and has his own contradictory interpretation of Scripture.

William Miller (Seventh Day Adventist) proclaimed that the World would end in 1843. Many of his followers committed suicide. Miller subsequently set other arbitrary dates, which came and went without the World coming to an end. We are still here.

We have other modern day prophets who have led their flock to destruction, namely Jim Jones and David Koresh.

Do the Followers of Henry Tudor believe that John Knox is wrong? What then of Mary Baker Eddy? Does she have the one true faith to follow to the exclusion of all others? What her faith teaches is contrary to most others. What about Joseph Smith, has he not declared that the other Protestant Faiths are in error? What then of Bullinger, and C. P. Jones, Richard Allen, John Cotton, Charles Taze Russell, Jim Jones, and David Koresh and many, many others. Each one of them proclaimed their own brand of Scriptural interpretation.

The Lutheran Church has itself has fragmented, and each Synod having a different interpretation of Scripture, Plus none of them follow the theology of Martin Luther. The Anglican / Episcopal Faith is no different, and is again on the verge of a schism due to a conflict in interpretation of Scripture.

Here are some of the different teachings by various Protestant Faiths:

> Some will acknowledge that Christ chose Peter as the Head of His Church
> Others will deny this, and find many differing reasons to deny him
>
> Some Faiths will accept the Holy Eucharist as a Sacrament
> Other will only accept the Eucharist as a Ritual
>
> Some will accept infant Baptism
> Others will limit it to consenting adults

Some Faiths accept Divorce and the right to remarry
Others will not

Some have accepted homosexuality as a Christian life style
Others say it is an abomination

Some will accept the Holy Trinity Three Persons in One God
Others will deny this

Some teach Predestination
Others cannot accept this

Some will teach that any one can interpret Scripture
Others say otherwise

Some teach that Faith Alone is sufficient for Salvation
Others say Good Works is sufficient for Salvation

Some will prohibit dancing and drinking wine is a sin
Others deny this teaching

Some will say that Jesus had siblings through Mary
Others will teach that Jesus was Mary's only child

Some will deny the existence of Hell
Other Faiths will proclaim that there is a Hell

Some will condemn statues as Idolatry
Others will accept statues as a means of remembrance

Some will accept Mary as the Earthly Mother of God
Others will not accept her as such

Some Faiths will accept Mary as a Perpetual virgin
Other Faith deny this

Most have accepted Jesus as the Son of God and is God
Other find fault with this teaching

Some Faiths will approve of Holy Matrimony between homosexuals
Most others Faiths decry this as an abomination

Some Faiths say that a valid marriage is between one man and one woman
There are those today that disagree with this concept

A few approve of praying to a Saint to intercede for our needs
Most others call this Blasphemy

Some Faiths say that Saturday is the Lord's Day
Most other Faiths find fault with this concept

Several Faiths approve of Women priests/ministers
Others cannot accept this teaching saying it violates Scripture

Some Faiths demand Tithing
Most others do not demand that you tithe, only give what you can

Some Faiths will condemn abortion
Other Faiths will say it is a Woman's right

Needless to say there are many other differences within the Protestant movement. We could go on and on with regard to the vast differences in Protestant Theology. Two facets are common. One is that they all have a different interpretation of Scripture, and two; they are all united in their Anti-Catholic rhetoric.

What I found most interesting in my studies regarding religion is that most Protestant Denominations do not believe in praying to a Saint. Some even say that that is sacrilegious. They claim that by praying to a person (Saint) you are honoring a person as a god. Nothing can be further that the truth. In praying to a Saint, we believe that the Saint is in the presence of God, and we ask the Saint to intercede for us with God.

At one time, while discussing the practice of Catholics praying to Saint Anthony to aid us in finding a lost article, with a Protestant couple, the young man implied that this was the work of the devil. He was somewhat taken aback when his wife did admit that she had prayed to St Anthony asking help in retrieving a lost article, and she did find it. Work of the devil?

Now let us look at the practice of Praying to a Saint. In the Old Testament, there are many passages relating to God communicating with us mere mortals. Also several times Angels have been the source of communication. After the Resurrection of Jesus, there has been no note of God directly communicating with us mortals. However there are many instances of Saints and the Blessed Virgin contacting individual here on Earth.

Perhaps the reason that the Protestants deny the contact between Saints and mortals is that none of them has had that experience. It seems only Catholics have been contacted.

There is a famous expression, "they cannot see the forest for the trees". This is what I detect in Protestant thinking. They are very, very good in proclaiming Scripture, Chapter and Verse. However Most of the proclamations were from the Old Testament or from the Epistles. Many times the passages were taken out of context.

A very good example of this is, when I had questioned a Nondenominational couple regarding the validity of divorce, the young lady came up with a passage from the Old Testament, completely ignoring the directive of Jesus. I asked "who do we follow, Moses or Jesus?" There was no lucid reply, only more rhetoric regarding Scripture from the Old Testament.

I have been most fortunate in that I have been able to travel, and to visit several churches, where I could see the results of many, many miracles attributed to Saints. I have seen pillars festooned with crutches from individual who believe that they have been cured thru the intercession of a Saint. I myself have been witness to what I firmly believe was not one but several miracles as a result of praying to a Saint to intercede for us with our Heavenly Father.

Many Protestant Faiths denounce the display of pictures of Saints, and even a crucifix, claiming this is idolatry. What is the difference between that and a picture of a loved one? Is the picture of our baby or a departed loved one idolatry? I think not! It is a reminder of one we love and want to keep in our hearts.

Just as an invalid uses a crutch to walk, so we as Christians us a crucifix or a rosary, to aid us in keeping Our Lord in our hearts and our minds.

With this in mind I find it interesting that some Presbyterian and Methodist churches now display the icon of the Blessed Virgin. The reasoning for that is to entice Latinos into their Fold. Latinos have a very strong affinity for the Blessed Virgin, Our Lady of Tepeyac. The churches not only have an icon of the Blessed Virgin, but also pictures of Her in their offices where they meet prospective members.

Already we are seeing a break in the ranks of some Presbyterians and Methodists churches regarding the Virginity of Mary, the Blessed Virgin. Rev Donald Charles Lacy a Methodist Minister called for the acceptance of the Virgin Mary's *intercessory role with God*, and accepting the Immaculate Conception and the Bodily Assumption of Mary into Heaven.

Today there are a growing number of Protestant Divinity schools that are teaching Marianology along with the Perpetual Virginity of the earthly mother of Jesus (God). Her picture, icons of the Blessed Virgin adorns their offices. Many Protestant Ministers now have Her picture in their offices and within their churches.

In Ohio, Rev. Maguire has stated that we (Protestants) are **open to change, regarding Mary.**

Change?

What the Rev Maguire really means is that there is a RETURN to the *original* theology of the Founding Fathers of the Reformation. ALL of the Founding Fathers believed that Mary, the Earthly Mother of God, was a Perpetual Virgin.

The Episcopalian Church, in South America, has used the subterfuge of their Masses being similar to the Catholic Mass to gain converts. The Episcopal Faith is not as strict as the Catholic Faith, and so it invites "lukewarm" Catholics to join their ranks.

II

Contradictions of the Protestant Faiths

"Thou Art Peter, and Upon This Rock, I Will Build My Church"

Every Bible has this passage. Yet every Protestant Faith will find some excuse to deny or ignore it. Some say that Jesus changed His mind. Others will say it was to Peter only, and only for that generation. The "newest" effort at denial is, that the "correct" interpretation of the *rock* is "pebble"

How absolutely ridiculous! Are they saying that the correct interpretation of that passage is "Thou art Peter, and upon this pebble I will build my Church"? The Protestants cannot agree amongst themselves how to interpret this passage.

Did not Our Lord say "Not all who say Lord, Lord, will enter the Kingdom of Heaven, but ONLY those who do the Will of My Father! On the Last Day, many will come to Me and say to Me, Lord did we not prophesy in Thy Name. And cast out Devils in THY name, and do mighty works in Thy name."

Does not Our Lord respond, "I never knew you, depart from Me you Evil doers."

In His Parable, Our Lord has made many references to the **"ROCK"**. Our Lord has said the "Every one, then that hears these Words of Mine, and does them, is like a Wise man who has built his house upon a **ROCK,** and the winds came and the rains fell and blew and beat against the House, but:
IT DID NOT FALL

Did not Our Lord say further, "And everyone who hears these Words of Mine, and does not do them, is like a man who builds his house upon <u>sand</u>." You ALL know what happens to the house built on sand.

We have but to look at the history of the Protestant Movement. The Church that Luther established no longer exists. Not only are there three separate Churches teaching three different interpretations of Scripture, but NONE of them are following the Basic Tenets espoused by Martin Luther.

"I give to you the Keys to the Kingdom of Heaven"

Here again we have another contradiction. This was said to Peter by Our Lord. It is **Scripture,** and still our Protestant friends will deny this passage as a Command to Peter, from God. The question I would ask is "if Our Lord gave Peter the Keys to the Kingdom of Heaven, (which I believe) then does that not give Peter the authority to pass the Keys on to his successors? Who among you will believe that Our Savior did not provide for the continuation of His Faith (Church).

This is Scripture, and it is denied by almost every Protestant.

> Whose Sins You Shall Forgive,
> They are Forgiven
> Whose Sins You Shall Retain,
> They Are Retained

Here again we a passage from Scripture, which is bestowing authority upon His Apostles (Church). The authority thus bestowed, has given His Church the power to forgive sins, and withhold forgiveness. Here again our Protestant friends will deny this passage in Scripture. They would have us believe that Jesus established a Church that had no authority.

To whom was this authority given? Was it not Peter? Again we go back to the start, and we have almost all Protestants denying anything pertaining to Peter. I would ask, "why did

Jesus change Simon's name to Peter (Rock)? Peter, a Rock upon which His Church would be built. To deny Peter, is to deny Scripture.

What else did Our Lord say regarding Peter? When Peter had replied to Jesus question as to "who do you believe I am?" Peter responded that He was the Son of God. Did not Our Lord say, of Peter,

"This knowledge does not come from man, but from my Heavenly Father".

If then, if Peter's knowledge of Jesus Divinity came from Heaven, and not man, how can anyone then deny his (Peter) authority, and the authority of his successors (Pope)?

The Gates of Hell Shall Not Prevail Against It

Here again we have a denial of Scripture by our Protestant brethren. Not only did Jesus establish Peter as the Head of His Church here on Earth, BUT He said it would withstand the Powers of the Devil. To my thinking, if the Catholic Church has failed, then this is a contradiction of Christ's Proclamation. If He is wrong, then He cannot be God. Therefore to deny His Church, is to deny the Divinity of Jesus.

This I cannot do.

False Prophets Will Come and Preach in My Name Do Not heed them.

With the Catholic Church, we have a Faith that was established at the time of Christ and has been functioning for over one thousand, five hundred years, and then along comes a dissident who says that the Catholic Church is wrong in their Theology. But does it stop there. Heck No! Then despite, the warnings of Calvin, **thousands** of "Christian" sects have arisen, each one expounding a diverse theology, which they *claim* is the Word of God. How can this be? If the Catholic Church is wrong, then the Protestants are correct.

But which one?

With all the diverse teaching of the various Protestant Faiths, they all cannot be right, so it is only logical that some, if not ALL protestant Faiths are in error. Which Protestant Faith will step forward and proclaim that they are the One True <u>continuation</u> of the Church established by Our Lord.

Our Lord had promised that the Holy Spirit would be with His Church for ALL time. Therefore I ask of ALL Protestants Faiths, show us where the Holy Spirit has been with YOU since the Time of Christ. <u>You cannot do so</u>.

There are a plethora of so called "Christian" sects, who proclaim that they are preaching the Word of God, and yet preaching a theology completely contrary to every other Protestant Faith. Not One Protestant Faith has the intestinal fortitude to unmask these charlatans and call then what they are. Heretics!

When I asked of an assistant pastor at a nondenominational church in the Chicago suburbs, "how do I find the One True Teaching of Jesus". His reply was to "Pray to the Holy Spirit for guidance". This was a subtle admission that his church was not the one true teaching of Our Lord.

I find it disturbing that various Protestant sects will condemn the Catholic church, and yet keep silent on those among them that deny the Holy Trinity, and even the Holy Eucharist.

There Shall Be One Fold and One Shepherd

Once again we have a bit on consternation. How can there be One Fold (Church) when there are so very many (twenty five thousand or more) differences as to what is meant by the Words of Jesus. Those of the Protestant Faiths that I have addressed, come up with basically the same mantra. *Jesus is the Shepherd and Scripture is the Fold.* How can this be? The utterance was issued to Peter, when He proclaimed Peter as the Head of His Church. This is like a State saying that "yes we believe in the

Constitution, but we do not believe in it's interpretations. We have the duty to interpret it as WE see fit". What a fallacy!

Supposing the State took exception to the phrase "all men are created equal". The State would then say that this does NOT apply to women as the Constitution does NOT mention women. How ludicrous! Yet this is how many Protestant are interpreting Scripture. They interpret Scripture with an Anti-Catholic bias.

One Fold, One Shepherd MUST mean, <u>One Church and One Interpretation of Scripture.</u> Not mix mashes of contrary interpretations of Scripture. I have yet to have a Protestant come forth and show where the Holy Spirit has been with their Faith from the time of Jesus, until the present time. They haven't because they cannot.

What God Has Joined Together, Let No Man Put Asunder

Here we have the greatest contradiction in the Protestant community. In my humble experience, in discussing this passage from Scripture, the Protestant will look me straight in the eye, and start quoting from the Old Testament, chapter and verse where divorce is permitted. They will also quote a passage from the Epistles. However, the passage is most often taken out of context. They completely ignore what Christ had said.

Another defense of their repudiation of this Passage is, that <u>these are modern time, and the world has changed,</u> and the Church must change to properly minister to its people. They will add further that Christianity has failed mankind, and it is time to change.

My reply is that mankind is failing Christianity. The Protestant movement is diluting Scripture in an effort to entice additional membership.

From the beginning, God made man and woman. When He sent them from Eden, He told them to go forth and multiply. As a result of the relaxing of the marriage vows by the various Protestant sects, we have seen a severe decline in respect for marriage.

Fully one third of babies born in the United States today, are to unmarried women. Many are barely teenagers. We have babies having babies. Abortion is rampant. Fully 25% of women of childbearing age are infected with a sexually transmitted disease. As new drugs are discovered to combat these diseases, more and more deadly diseases are discovered. Many women and men are permanently afflicted by these maladies. The results are that many are made sterile, and many children are born deformed.

Marriage should be based on Love not Lust. It seems that the criteria for marriage today are, "how good is he/she in bed". "Sample it before you buy it". There appears to be little thought regarding home and family. It is more like obtaining a sex partner. As a result, the offspring from these unions are more often than not, emotionally affected. Fathers and mothers are drifting back and forth between spouses. This is utterly confusing to the children, and denying them stability.

Many will say that marriage today is a failure, and half of the marriage ends in divorce. This in and of itself may be true, but:

What is the rest of the story?

For those who marry and make a firm commitment to marriage, such as a religious ceremony, taking the vow to "forsake all others" and committing their lives to Our Lord, and raising a family and living by those vows, the failure rate is perhaps, one or two in ten, not 5 in ten. Of those who have a failed marriage, many will adhere to Christ's teaching and refrain from entering into another marriage or sexual relationship out side of marriage.

Today, in my humble opinion, most marriages are based on lust not love. What we have seen in very many divorces are that the former spouses will invariably marry another person who possesses the same traits as their former spouse.

Many individual today will marry "on the spur of the moment". The feeling is that they can always have an opportunity to dissolve the union. A woman or a man may leave their spouse, but what of the children. Children are shuttled back and forth between former spouses. Children have a mother and a father; they are never a former father, or a former mother, like the spouses are former husband and former wife.

With the decline in respect for marriage, many couples tends to cohabitate. Yet the failure rate of cohabitating couples is greater that the divorce rate among married couples. What is the grand result of the cohabitation? Many women are left with children as the male moves on to greener pastures. Many women choose to abort their "mistake". This results in millions of babies being slaughtered.

The Protestant Faiths seem to ignore the admonition against fornication. When I asked "is not cohabiting fornication"? The usual reply is that they cannot find reference to Fornication in Scripture, and if it is not mentioned in Scripture, they can ignore it.

They have but to really look, as it is mentioned more than once in Scripture.

Fornication, the last time I looked in the dictionary, was classed as unmarried sex.

Perhaps, what is written above is why the Protestant Churches do not accept marriage as a Sacrament.

For a Man to lay with a Man as with a Woman Is an Abomination.

Here we have, what is becoming the start of a great schism within the Protestant Community. Many Protestant Faiths are succumbing to the Politically Correct atmosphere permeating the world today. The very Churches that castigate the Catholic Church for "alleged" failures, are very silent on their Brethren who are deviating from their own Teachings.

Today the Anglican/Episcopalian communities are at a crossroads. The Anglican Community decries the drift of the Episcopalian Community toward accepting homosexuality as an acceptable life style, even to the extent of offering Holy Matrimony for the same sex couples.

The Episcopalian Faith is itself divided, and on the verge of a Schism, that will create yet another "Christian" Church.

Here again we come to yet another contradiction within the Protestant community. How can they claim to be of "One Fold" when there are so many contradictions within their Communities?

One Faith says that homosexuality is ordained from God, Another says it is an Abomination

"Any Plowman can Interpret Scripture"
Martin Luther

One of the pronouncements made by Martin Luther, following his schism from the Catholic Church was that every plowman could interpret Scripture. This, in effect, is saying that anyone can interpret Scripture. Let us equate this with modern times so we can rationalize this.

In essence, Holy Scripture is to Religion what our Constitution is to us Americans. If we then accept Luther's premise regarding interpretation of Scripture, we must then accept that any person in the United States can interpret the Constitution.

What a fallacy! With the "Bill of Rights" our constitution has about two dozen amendments. Can you or I "legally" interpret the Laws of the Land, or would some lawyer take us to a **Higher Court?** There are many different facets that have to be considered. What we believe or "wish" for is most often in conflict with the Law. You and I "think" we know the Law, but in reality we are most often wrong. This is why there are so many lawyers and so many different Courts.

There are many individual who take the phrase "All men are Created Equal", as to mean that only men are equal, not women, because the Constitution does not mention women. This in essence would deprive women of any Rights. There are many who subscribe to this interpretation. However it is the Supreme Court that interprets the Law, not the individual.

There is the letter of the Law and there is the Spirit of the Law. Who is there to decide which is Constitutional?

It is my belief that the Constitutional Legal system here in the United States is somewhat patterned after the Roman Catholic Church. In the Roman Catholic Church there is the Rota and there is the Apostolic Signatura, just as we have the Appeals Courts and the Supreme Court.

No where in the Protestant movement is there any kind of Theological Court. There are Synods that do meet from time to time, but to ALL appearances it has no real Authority.

A very good case in point is the problem besieging the Anglican/Episcopalian Faiths. Arch Bishop Rowan Williams just rings his hands and asks for patience, in an attempt to mollify both sides of the issue regarding ordination of homosexuals, plus the advocating Blessing a marriage between same sex couples.

The above sample is a very simple one. There are many more complex nuances of various laws. If we do not have the ability to interpret these nuances, how then can the uninformed individual (plowman) interpret Scripture? Imagine what it would be like, if we had no Supreme Court here in the United States? With everyone interpreting the law, as they believed it should be, there would be chaos, just as there is chaos in the Protestant Faiths.

Lets us equate the Reformation movement with the United States. What do you think would have happened, if the Confederate States had been successful in their secession? What is now the Continental United States would be at least three different Nations and more probably five Nations.

There would be the Confederate States, the Northern States East of the Mississippi, and either separate Western States. More probably Mexico and Great Britain would have moved into most of the Western areas. We would then be like Europe, a conglomeration of independent and diverse Nations. Russia or Great Britain would occupy Alaska and Hawaii would be part of the British Empire.

With this dilution of power here in the United States, where would the World be today. Who would have been there to stop Hitler? Who would there be to stop Tojo?

Japanese power would control the Pacific, and the Nazi regime would control Europe. The "Rights of Man" as we know them today would not exist.

Both Hitler and Tojo were anti Christian and anti Jew, so what do you imagine what this World would be like today.

America was built on the knowledge and efforts of many diverse peoples working as a **single unit**.

E Pluribus Unum
One from Many

What we have in Protestant Christianity today is,

Many from One

So this is what has happen as a result of the Protestant secession from the Catholic Church. The Protestants have diluted the Word of God and have diluted the Power of Christianity. Christianity has always been under attack by the Moslem Faith, but even more so today. The Moslem does not fear any and all of the various Protestant sects, but they are apprehensive of the Power of the Catholic Church.

12

Divide and Conquer, Dilute and Destroy

Who can deny that the Christian Teachings have been diluted? Ask any Protestant if their Church is the One True Church of Jesus Christ, and they will reply that they all are Teaching God's Word.

How can this be when they ALL disagree with each other? The only thing that bonds the Protestant Faiths is their Anti-Catholic agenda. Here we have today, many of the young turning away from "organized "religion but still looking for something spiritual. Most are ending in Faith like cults. Many are foregoing any form of religion.

The anti religion community has grown so bold as to be making a concerted effort to remove all vestiges of Christianity from public schools, meetings sports events and even to have it removed from the "Pledge of Allegiance". Pressure is put upon various Super Markets and other retailers, to discourage their employees from rendering the greeting of "Merry Christmas". Instead the employees are instructed to say "Happy Holidays".

In our public schools, the children are no longer allowed to sing Christmas carols. Nativity displays are prohibited from any public building. Even the address to Congress, given by former President Franklin Delano Roosevelt, on December 8th, 1941, in which he asked for a declaration of war against the Japanese Nation, as a result has of their sneak attack on Pearl Harbor,

Hawaii, has been edited in official National archives. When President closed his address, he finished with the words

"We will gain the inevitable triumphant"

Missing are the final words, removed from the archives:

"So help us God"

I was present in my High School assembly, and heard the speech, and he did finish with "So help us God".

Public school athletes are no longer allowed to pray before a game. A valedictorian, at a high school graduation, had the microphone snatched from her as she was giving her address to the assembly, because she mentioned that she wanted to thank God for her success. Teachers are no longer allowed to wear any item of a religious nature, especially if it is Christian in context.

On last Christmas Eve, I went to the local Jewel to obtain a few last minute necessities for our Christmas meal. As I was being checked out, I greeted the cashier with "Merry Christmas". She replied, "Happy Holiday". I asked why she replied that way. Her retort was that she did not want to offend other religions or atheists. Finally, I asked her if she would be working the following day. Her reply was "no she had the day off". Here again I asked why she had the day off, as it was not her regular day off. She replied that this was because it was Christmas.

You all know what my reply to this discussion was.

Merry Christmas, and a Happy New Year.

It is a sad commentary on our beliefs today. In ancient times, Christians would go to their deaths, rather then to deny Christ. Today, lukewarm Christians are even afraid to say Merry Christmas; for fear that they might offend someone or even lose their jobs. Christmas is a Holiday celebrated through out the World. Our calendar is based upon the birth of Christ and was established by Pope Gregory XII., on February 24, 1582. This is a calendar that is in use throughout the World today. A Calendar established by the <u>Catholic Church</u>.

All the while Christianity is under attack, and the Moslem Faith is gaining strength. Today there are two major Faiths, Islam and Catholicism, each having over a Billion followers. While the Protestant Faiths are diluting the Word of God, Islam is gaining strength. It's foothold in Europe is growing and it is now gaining a foothold here in America.

Is Protestantism an unintentional ally of Islam? The Arabs have a "saying":

The enemy of my enemy is my friend.

In all their preaching about theology, the Protestants are ignoring the variances within their own Religions; their main mantra is anti Catholic, anti Pope. While we Christians are fighting amongst ourselves, radical Islam is gaining converts in Europe, and America. Protestants deem to ignore the brother religions that teach a contrary theology.

Despite the fact that Catholicism is under attack by Islam and the Protestant movement, plus the recent sex scandals, the Catholic Church is still gaining more members that all the Protestants Faiths. Main line Protestant Faiths are plagued with a declining membership. The only Faith that has a higher percentage of growth is the Mormon Faith. However their membership is miniscule compared with Catholicism.

Catholics, Mormons, and Islam are strict religions, and yet this seems to be what the populace wants. As the Protestants ease their "rules" and theology, they in turn lose members, either through parts of their congregation leaving for another Faith, or, as many have, lose faith in Christianity and Religion in general.

We have, with the Lutheran Faiths, yes Faiths; if you are unhappy with one Lutheran Faith you can always join another, which has basically the same, but a slightly different theology. Very few of the Lutherans, know that their Church does NOT teach the Theology of Martin Luther. It has been compromised, diluted and in many aspects ignored. I would dare say that many of its Pastors do not realize it themselves. The one single carry over from the time of Luther is the Anti Pope mantra.

The Protestant Faiths are somewhat like the Chicago Weather. If one does not like the weather here in Chicago, the saying is, "just wait a short while and it will change" .So it is with Protestantism, the various Faiths are in a constant state of flux. What is accepted today as Scripture will by tomorrow be discarded. The Protestant Faith is a very adaptable Faith. If you don't like what one teaches, then you go to another, which could be teaching a completely contrary theology, yet it is, and you are, a Protestant.

Since the time of Wesley, Methodists have morphed, divided, united and are today in a state of flux. The theology of the Methodist Faith is like the Lutheran Faith in that it does not come anywhere near the theology of Wesley. The big question today is that of acceptance of a homosexual life style as a Christian life style.

With the Presbyterians, what was once anti Marianology, is today venerating Her, in an attempt to influence Latinos.

As to the Nondenominational Faiths, there you have a smorgasbord of Theology. Nondenominational Faiths have a plethora a various and sundry Scriptural teachings. Therefore you "pick" the belief that suits you and "go" with that Church. I have seen where an individual or a family will embrace a Nondenominational Faith due to the charisma of the Pastor.

"Many False Prophets will come and preach in My name"

Our Lord warned us about false prophets, and warned us NOT to listen to them. In the Parable of the "Sowing of the Seeds", Christ warned that many seeds would fall among the weeds and be choked. The fallacy of Protestantism is in their belief that they are adhering to the Word of God. How can this be, when there are some many <u>diverse teachings</u>, only one teaching can be right!

Religion is in a decline in the Western World, because of the infighting among Catholics and Protestants. All the while, Islam is spreading through the world. Islam controls South West Asia, North Africa, and area of the Pacific, plus part of Eastern and Western Africa.

When Islam controls the Government, Christianity is "locked out". In many of these countries controlled by Islam, the importing of a Bible or a crucifix or even a rosary is a crime against the State, and punishable by a term in prison, or worse.

If a Moslem would convert to Christianity, They would be subject to execution.

Desecration of the Koran, or even to treat the "Book" with disrespect, is a crime, punishable by death. Yet we "Christians" stand idly by as an "artist" will cover an icon of the Blessed Virgin with animal dung or put a Crucifix in a vat of urine. These acts are considered expressions of Art. Anti Christian movies and plays are in vogue today. Books filled with lies, distortions, half truths are classified as historical fact, when in reality they are fiction.

The irony of all this is, that to cast aspersions against a Christian Religion, is allowed as "Freedom of Religion", and "Freedom of Speech". However if anyone so much as tears a leaf from the Koran, or make a public comment denigrating Islam, they are subject to procesecution <u>for a "Hate" crime here in the United States</u>.

Degrading Christianity is Freedom of Speech and Religion. Denigrating Islam is considered AND is prosecuted as A Hate Crime.

In Islam, women are not coequal with men. Men are obliged to pray 5 times a day, and their time of fasting will last a month. It is also an obligation for a true Moslem to partake of a Hajj, which is to make a pilgrimage to Mecca in their life time.

With very many Protestant Faiths, it is not mandatory to attend services, and there is no requirement for a period of fasting.

What does it take to be a Protestant minister? Christianity is continually being diluted by the proliferation of Store

Front Churches (Nondenominational). There are virtually no requirements to obtain a Theological degree for any individual who wants to "start" a new Faith.

For a few dollars, I obtained a Certificate of Ordination, with ALL the powers therein. I can legally officiate at a wedding, which will be legally binding, not only here in the U S A but also through most of the World. For a few dollars I received a Doctorate in Religious study and a PHD in Theology. To push to "envelope" further, I requested an appointment as a Bishop, which, with a few paltry dollars was accomplished. All the while, there was not testing, no background searches, no schooling, *and just "thirty pieces of silver"*.

The attack on Christianity is taking part on many fronts. In Sweden and Canada, several ministers have been threatened with prosecution because they preached that Homosexuality was contrary to God's Law. Catholic Hospitals are also threatened with legal action for refusing to perform abortions. In Boston, Catholic Charities may no longer participate in Adoption Services, because Catholic Charities will not and cannot (Theologically) service homosexual couples seeking to adopt.

Another attack on Christianity is an effort to revise the calendar. In many circles the change is made from A D to C E. The reference to our year is 2006 C E (Common Era), not 2006 A D (Anno Domini) the year of our Lord.

Our Good Lord had said "they have eyes to see and cannot see". We cannot see the cancer of Islam that is growing, and where Islam gains a foot hold, religious freedom ceases to exist.

In West Central Africa and in Indonesia Moslems are attacking and killing Christian families. Schools are burned and students are being raped, and the Christian community stands mute to this anti Christian carnage, because we are too busy fighting amongst ourselves. Many individuals will point to the conflict in Northern Ireland between Catholics and Protestants where many were killed on both sides.

Pope John Paul II did go to Ireland and did admonish the Catholic to cease in these violent acts. I personally know of no prominent Protestant figure that did the same. As a result of the visit by the Pope, violence has appreciably diminished.

To date, I know of no prominent Moslem Cleric or Imam, who publicly deplores the violence against Christians and calls for an end of the attacks. Unless I am sadly mistaken, the Koran mandates death to Infidels, (Christians). The same Koran mandates death to any Moslem that converts to Christianity.

Some apologist will point to some of the few a Christian churches that exist within various Moslem Countries. This, to me, is tantamount to what transpired here in the Southern States at the early stages of the Civil Rights movement. Businesses would point to their "token Niger" as an act of compliance within the Law.

When Islam gains control of the Government, the "door" to Christianity and all other Faiths is closed.

Egyptian Clerics have stated that Islam will succeed without a Crusade. At present the Christian population in Europe is diminishing due to immigration, contraception or abortion. The Moslem population in Europe is growing most notably in Germany, Austria, Spain, France and Great Britain. Already, in Britain and France, Moslems are demanding to have their own legal system (Sharia).

For a barrel of oil, we here in the West are overlooking these transgressions. Should someone vandalize a Masque, they would be charged with a Hate Crime, but desecration of a religious Christian object is considered "Art", or freedom of Religion and freedom of Speech.

Islam claims that the West, especially Europe will be an easy target, and then followed by the Americans.

There are several reasons for this belief, which I would say are valid:

1. The division among Christians, thereby diluting their Faith, and thwarting resistance to Islam

2. Contraception, thereby reducing the size of the family, or encouraging many couples to avoid a family
3. Abortion is an abomination in that it not only destroys a life, but also dilutes the values of life.
4. Ambition. The Western World has replaced the value of the family, with the value of luxuries

Moslem scholars have stated that the West is more concerned with obtaining a bigger car, a larger T V, a roomier house, and an exotic vacation. They claim the time will come soon, due to the infighting of Christians, thereby diluting their faith and resistance.

Much has been made, of the utterances by the President of Iran, Mahmoud Ahmadinejad regarding the desire to eliminate Israel. Hardly any notice has been given to a much more serious threat. President Ahmadinejad has called upon the followers of Islam to prepare to *"take over the World"*. He has prophesied that Islam will conquer the World.

Christianity has been severely weakened by the Protestant Reformation. Calvin had called upon the followers of Martin Luther to join in a single universal interpretation of Scripture. Failure to do so, Calvin warned, would dilute Christian Theology and so it has happened.

Dilute and Destroy

The continual diluting of Christianity is undermining the Teachings of Our Lord. Most Protestant justify their actions by condemning the Catholic Church, and yet, Protestants have no ONE source as a replacement of the Catholic Church.

The ultimate goal of Islam is the elimination of all other religions. **The Protestant movement**, by diluting the Word of God, is in my opinion, is weakening Christianity, and in so doing, **is aiding and abetting the growth of Islam.**

Over the years I have heard a great many *excuses* as to why someone has joined a Protestant Faith. But no one has given me a valid *reason*. There are those who have gone to a Protestant service because they are entertained by the music, or in some instances, the theatrics. There are those who are mesmerized by the speaker, and others who just love the music.

Can you imagine Our Lord giving His Sermon on the Mount, followed by music provided by "The Apostle 12" band, and free meals? Or was it just simple words, spoken from the heart? Do we attend Mass (services) to be entertained, or to Hear the Word of God?

I have met many Protestants who "claim" that they have learned more from a Protestant service then they had learned from a Catholic Mass.

But what did they learn? As the street vernacular says:
"Different Strokes for Different Folks".

Each Protestant Faith has a VASTLY different interpretation of Scripture. So what is a Protestant learning?

Homosexuality is an abomination
A homosexual is created in God's image and is permissible

Divorce is prohibited
Divorce is permitted in today's society

Baptism is necessary for Salvation
Baptism is not mandated in Scripture

A priest/minister has the authority to forgive sins
Only God can forgive sins

Partaking of alcohol and dancing are sins
Moderate use of alcohol and dancing are permitted

Peter was appointed as Head of Jesus Church
Peter was told to go away by Jesus

The Blessed Virgin is the Mother of Jesus (God)
Mary was just another woman

Fasting is mandatory at certain times
Fasting is not necessary

Tithing is mandated
Tithing is not necessary

Marriage must be preformed by a Priest/minister of the Church
Marriage rite can be preformed by anyone.

The above is just the **"tip of the iceberg"**. There are many many more differences within the Protestant movement. There are many individuals who have joined the Catholic Faith, because of the heroic actions of some individual. There are also, many who have left the Faith because of the dastardly actions, or implied actions of a priest or other member of the Faith. But what is the Truth?

A lesson I learned, from a good Nun at St Williams School in Chicago, was regarding three blind men being taken to the Zoo to "see" an elephant. The first felt the trunk, and said the elephant was long, thick and wiggly. The second, felt the leg of the elephant, and said he was tall and round. The third felt the tail, and said the elephant was small, thin and spirally. They all thought they had found the true elephant, yet they were all partially right, but mostly wrong. Not one of the blind men found the true elephant, just as Protestants, have not found the One True Church. With Protestants, they "see" what they want to "see".

13

Sins of the Clerics

Many individual have left the Catholic Church and "found" a new Faith because of the Sex Scandals that rocked Christendom in the early 21st century. These individuals, and society in general, completely ignored the fact that for every Catholic priest who was accused of sexual abuse, there were **two or more** Protestant ministers who perpetrated the same crimes. It appears that only the accusations against Catholic priest make the Front Pages of the media, and are prominently displayed on TV. Meanwhile, the same immoral acts by Protestant clergy are either ignored or relegated to the "back" pages of the media.

A case in point is the charge against a Catholic priest in Chicago in February 2006. For several WEEKS TV channel 9 (WGN) highlighted the accusations against the same priest using the same "file" film footage. This "breaking" new went on for several weeks, with nothing new being added to the charges against him. At the same time, two Negro ministers from two different churches were accused of sexual abuse. There was no in depth interview of the ministers or their congregations.

It was **"One and Done"**.

There has been, to my knowledge, no follow-up, no explanation as to the disposition of the charges. All three cases were handled differently by the Media. Could it be that in one case it was a Caucasian Catholic priest, and the others were Negro Protestant Clergy? ALL sexual abuse by clergy should be equally highlighted by the Media, and ALL abusers should be incarcerated, and removed from the Ministry FOR LIFE.

When you talk to people today, they have the perception that the abuse of children is paramount within the Catholic Church. And seem totally unaware that the same problem exists with regard to Protestant Clergy. Surveys by independent agencies have shown that among Catholic Priests, the rate of abuse was 0.8%, while the "recorded" rate of abuse was 1.8% of the Protestant Clergy and staff. When you consider that there are well over three times as many Protestant Ministers as there are Catholic Priests, it would indicate that the rate of abuse by Protestant Clergy is very much higher that that of the Catholic Priests.

Very many cases of sexual abuse by Protestant clergy, is investigated "in House", and punishment, if any, is also handled "in House", with no National notoriety.

Let me say here, that there is no excuse what so ever, for the sexual abuse of women and children, especially those who look to a religious community for guidance.

"Two Wrongs Do Not Make A Right"

All my life I have heard of the "allegation" of wrong during by the Catholic Church. Never once had I heard of the same allegations regarding the Protestant Faiths. This is the reason why I bring into the open, the "sins" of the Protestant Clergy. Most instances of abuse by Protestant minister are confined to local media, and very seldom do these accusations make "Front Page" headlines.

While the Chicago Tribune will "Front Page" an accusation regarding a Catholic Priest, the same newspaper will relegate to the back pages of the Friday edition, stories regarding Protestant ministers accused of the same heinous acts. These "news" items will usually be a very small paragraph or two.

Over the past several years I have come upon some of the following items of sexual abuse by Protestant ministers, as recorded in *local* news papers and *social agencies*.

There are numerous incidents of Protestant ministers using Scripture to entice female members to commit adultery with them. What various ministers have done is to use the parable of the "Lost Sheep" to justify this heinous act. The minister would explain that by "sinning" they become a "lost" sheep, and by repenting, they make God happy.

Does not Scripture say there is more joy in Heaven, regarding the "return" of a lost sheep, then there is for the 99 who remained faithful? This gambit has been used very many times, and still I have not heard of ANY Protestant organization dispensing punishment upon the cleric. When the minister is "found out", he both repents and asks for forgiveness, or like the Bedouin, he folds his tent and moves to another pasture. My own survey has shown to me, that up to 10% of nondenominational Churches in a years time, have either cease to exist, move or change their name.

Couple this, with the fact there is no formal education or theological training for ANY individual, to start his/her own Church (Religion). There is No governing body, within the Protestant movement to govern or regulate nondenominational clergy.

Anyone can call themselves Minister (Reverend) and very many do. Some may be left their homeland for more fertile field, and may even be a "recovering" dope addicts or alcoholic. Some may even have a criminal record. Some "ministers" will pay their 30 pieces of silver to obtain a "certificate" stating they are a Minister. I should know, I have more that one. Several will take it one step further and have them selves called "Bishop". Again, I should know because I have received a beautiful certificate declaring that **I am a duly authorized Bishop**. It only cost $25.00 to have a beautiful printed certificate from a diploma mill in Tennessee, which purports to be an International Nondenominational Church. There were no examinations or any testing of my theological knowledge.

What is equally disturbing is that a National survey has shown that up to 25% of Protestant Ministers is or has been engaged in adultery. Further, up to 50% of Protestant Ministers know of a colleague who is or has been involved in an adulteress relationship

Where is the judgment? Protestantism has NO central source of administering justice. As far as the media seems to be concerned, its *"One and Done", in reporting* the indiscretions of a member of the "cloth", except if happened to be a Catholic Priest. .

I can readily understand the media here in the Chicago area overlooking the case of a Lutheran Minister, in Arkansas, who abused several boys, and was transferred to another church, without informing the new congregation of the charges against the minister. The Lutheran Church settled this claim for several million dollars. After all, this was not news pertaining to the Chicago area. But what of the Nondenominational minister in the Mount Prospect area? Was he not accused of sexual abuse of a male minor? It seems that the defense of the "church" was that the State had no authority to be involved in Church matters. I heard of no action by any Child Welfare organization. It also appeared that a Mega Church in North West Chicagoland came to the aid of the *minister*, but what of the *child*.

Very many cases of child abuse are swept "under the rug" by many Nondenominational Churches. There are at least two methods of treating the accusations of abuse. One is to "blame" the child for tempting the minister and in turn punish the child. Mark well, the case of a young girl in the Elgin, Illinois area. When she was brought before her minister to recite her "claim" of sexual abuse, she in turn was beaten by the minister, and forced to *recant* her allegations.

If I am not mistaken, Illinois Law mandates that anyone who has knowledge of child abuse MUST report it to the authorities. Further investigation has proved that the child was not lying, and she was sexually abused. The perpetrator has been apprehended and is awaiting trial. As yet, I have not seen where the Minister has been charged with failure to report child abuse. Nor have I seen where the minister has been punished for his actions.

Incidents of this type are not an anomaly as I have found scores of cases of this type of conduct and worse, conducted by Protestant Clergy. None of these charges make the main line media. Usually, it is only recorded by the "neighborhood" news papers, where the incident occurred.

Another method of squelching complaints by Protestant Ministers and Church Elders is to threaten the complaining family with *shunning*. I have noted several cases where families have come before the Church Elders or Minister and threatened to go to the authorities. The families where told that if they did they would be driven from the Church and shunned. The families were told that the allegations were by a sinner against a Man of God. In fact there have been civil trials where the judge threw out the complaints, of a minor being abused by a Protestant minister, because the judge could not believe that a Man of God (Minister) could swear on a bible and then lie. So therefore the child MUST be lying.

Of the scores of complaints that I have uncovered, I have found , what I believe, is that for every family who defied the Church Elders or Minister and risked excommunication (shunning) three to four families accepted the decision of the Church., and no action was taken.

There are several cases where the Pastor has taken women into the sanctuary, and had them undress, and stand nude before him. The Pastor *quoted Scripture* to justify his actions. According to the Pastor, to be saved, one must bare their soul before God, and as he was a Man of God, if she wants to be *saved* she must comply. How, he asked, can one "bare their soul" if they are fully clothed. This action is not unique in itself; but has been perpetrated time after time in several churches. Many times, the end result is "just" looking at a naked woman, but very many incidents end in sexual activity. The "lost" sheep syndrome has worked on more than a few gullible women.

As of today, I have not seen where any of these allegations results in a rape accusation against a Protestant Minister, nor have I heard of any of these Ministers being chastised by

Church authorities. This may very well be that most Protestant Churches are autonomous, and as such are self governing.

There are very many individuals who protest my expose' of the criminal acts of Protestant clergy, saying that this does not justify the criminal acts by Catholic priests.

I heartily agree.

There can be no excuse or justification of the dastardly act by either Catholic Priest or Protestant Ministers. What I am trying to point out is the covert action by the secular press in emphasizing the "sins" of the Catholic Church, while giving only "token coverage to the "sins" of the Protestant Faiths. There can be no other explanation. With my limited time, talents and funds, I have been able to document well over 300 cases of sexual abuse involving over 350 Protestant clergy or staff.

Have you heard of any? I doubt it. However, I will bet you a dollar to a donut that you have heard of many cases of child abuse by Catholic clergy.

While a goodly number of women and young girls have been exploited by Protestant clergy, the vast majority of incidents involve young boys. Much has been made, and rightly so, of a former Catholic priest in Boston, who sodomized over a hundred boys. He was convicted and sent to prison, where he was murdered by an inmate. How many of you know of the Protestant minister who *admitted to sodomizing over one thousand boys and young men.* Where were the calls from society for accountability by his superiors? Who knows of any efforts to compensate these individuals, by providing counseling and financial help, which had been DEMANDED of the Catholic Church? His punishment could be construed as a "slap on the wrist".

A Baptist minister, while being a registered sex offender, was active within his church in giving counseling to those families in need, sexually abused a thirteen year old boy. When his family came to him for aid in finding shelter, the minister found a place for the mother and her other son. The minister then sexually abused the young boy. This REPEAT sexual abuse was noted in the main line media with a small three paragraph item on the: back pages" of the Chicago Tribune. I dare to say, that had this been a Catholic priest, the "item" would have made the front pages.

To date, I have not seen where the Baptist community has taken any actions regarding this *"minister"*.

A vast majority of the victims are young boys. How can this not be construed as a homosexual act?

Because Protestant ministers have committed well over three times as many heinous acts as Catholic priests, does not justify Catholic priests from doing the same. Again, I repeat, ALL act of sexual abuse should be exposed and published. The individual should be barred from any religious ministry.

Several Social agencies have stated that it is impossible to get a true figure regarding sexual abuse by Protestant Clergy, as very many of these incidents are handled "in house" and do not see the "light of Day". They also state that the recorded numbers are just the **"tip of the Ice berg"**.

14

THEOLOGY of the Founders of the Reformation.

In the early 1500's a so called "reform" movement began. There was Martin Luther, John Calvin, Huldrych Zwingali, Heinreich Bullinger, Henry VIII, and much later John Wesley. Each had their own agenda. And their "reform" movement has become known as the" Reformation." (Protestantism)

It was called Protestant because it was "protesting" the Teachings of the Catholic Church. There were a great many other heretical sects between 100 A D and 1500 A D.

Following is a list of some of them, not in chronological order:

APOLLINARIANS – They claimed that Jesus was not truly human
ARIANS – They claimed that Jesus was not God but a creation
COLLYRIDIANS – They sacrificed to Mary
DYNATISTS - They refused to readmit Apostate Christians. Those
who Renounced their faith, to avoid persecution
GNOSTICS – They believed that all mater was evil
MARCIONITES – They rejected the Gospels
MONACHIANISTS – They denied the Trinity, Three Persons in One God

MONTANISTS – They forbade marriage and wordily possessions
NESTORIANS – They claimed that Jesus had two personhoods
PELAGIANS – They denied Original Sin and the Need for Salvation

All these heretical sects withered and died, and had no effect upon Catholicism. What Luther and Henry had that the former heretics did not have was political (government) assistance. With Luther, it was jealousy on the part of the Germans who had desired the leadership of the Holy Roman Empire. With Henry, he was the King with full authority to do as he pleased. Henry broke from the Catholic Faith, because the Pope would not "bend" or change the Rules of the Church to accommodate Henry.

With Luther and Henry "starting" their own religion, others took heed and developed "faiths" of their own. Each new religion took some of Luther's Tenets and detracting others and then adding some of their own. As a result we now have well over twenty five thousand Protestant Faiths, each one teaching a contrary Theology, and yet claiming to be Teaching the True Scripture.

With the death of Pope John Paul II, Cardinal Ratzinger was elected Pope, taking the name of Benedict XVI. Very many Protestants expressed the view that the Catholic Church was continuing the "old" ways of Catholicism, and not adapting to "modern" times. Shall we look at back at what the four pillars of the Reformation taught?

Luther, Calvin, Henry Tudor and Wesley all believed in the Holy Trinity. Today a goodly number of their followers in the Protestant movement have "changed" their beliefs. Why was the belief in the Holy Trinity valid two thousand years ago? Why was it valid five hundred years ago? What theologian, in some of the Protestant Faiths has decreed that belief in the Holy Trinity is heresy? To teach something that is contrary to Scripture has got to be heresy! You cannot have it both ways.

What were the ORIGINAL beliefs of the Founders of Protestantism?

In 1580 the **"Book of Concord"** recorded the writings of Martin Luther, John Calvin, and Huldrych Zwingali. Also recorded were the **Schmalkaldic Articles (1537)** containing the beliefs of Martin Luther, John Calvin, Huldreich Zwingali, et al.

Martin Luther believed that Mary was the Mother of God. He taught that she was a Virgin at the birth of Christ, and remained a Virgin all her life. He was most emphatic that Mary the "Blessed Virgin" had no other children. He further taught the reference, in Scripture of *"Brothers and Sisters"* of Jesus were in keeping with the Arian meaning of *cousins*.

In Luther's sermon *"Sermon on John"*, Luther protested the LIE that was circulated about him regarding Mary. The Lie that was circulated was that he (Luther) had denied his firm belief in Mary **(Pelican 1539 Chapter 1-4)** in confronting this falsehood; Martin Luther reiterated his firm belief and his teachings that "Mary, the Mother of God, was in ALL ways a Virgin. She was a Virgin at the birth of Jesus and at her **Assumption** into Heaven, said Luther.

Luther had a disagreement with Calvin regarding Transubstantion (the Body and Blood of Christ being present in the Holy Eucharist). Calvin taught that the meaning of the presence of the Body and Blood of Christ in the Holy Eucharist was purely symbolic. Luther wrote that to accept this" belief as *symbolic* turns a Sacrament into a futile work of man, rather than a Grace and Blessing from God."

Here we see a Schism within a Schism. Beliefs of Protestants are contrary to Catholics, and beliefs of Protestants within Protestantism are contrary to each other.

No two Protestant Faiths teach the same Theology

How does this equate with Jesus command:
"There shall be One Fold, and One Shepherd".

Many, of the Protestant Faith, condemn the Catholics for praying to a Saint, asking the Saint to intercede for them. But then what of Martin Luther's beliefs?

In the *Augsburg Confession* (1530), which was sanctioned by Luther himself, in its **article 21**, recommended that "Saints must be kept in remembrance, so that our Faith may be strengthened. Moreover, their (Saints) "good works" are to be an example for us."

Many Protestants subscribe to the theology that "Faith Alone" will secure Salvation. Luther, the Founder of Protestantism had written and preached that:

"If Good Works do not follow Faith, then Faith in Jesus is dead".

John Calvin was just as adamant in his defense of the Perpetual Virginity of the "Blessed Virgin" the Mother of Jesus. Further Calvin took issue with Helvidius. Calvin called Helvidius ignorant in his (Helvidius) beliefs. Calvin stated that Helvidius reference to Christ's brothers and sisters was a misrepresentation of Scripture. Calvin agreed with Luther that the True interpretation in Scripture was and is **cousins or brethren.**

Both Luther and Calvin wrote and preached about the *"sins" of birth control*. In his *Commentary on Genesis* he spoke vehemently in opposition to artificial means of birth control He wrote:

"It is a horrible thing to pour out the *seed* besides the intercourse of a man and a woman. When a woman, in some way drives the seed out of the womb, through aids then it is rightly seen as a sin:

Unforgivable Sin"

Protestantism today, has refuted, ignored, altered and deviated from the theology of both Luther and Calvin, and still have the audacity to call these theologians as the Founders of their Faith. A Faith Protestants do not follow.

While Calvin is viewed by many historians as a religious extremist, he did prophesy what would happen to the Protestant movement, if it did not unite.

Calvin recognized *the absurdity of Protestant diverse theologies*, and said that its existence is an embarrassing **disproof of Protestantism's claims of preeminence over the Catholic Church.** Calvin added further:

**"The occasion of our dissentions speaks evil, and many are perplexed by our unintelligible disputations.
Satan is busy, sowing the seed of discord, by our Folly".**
John Calvin

**" From one Faith will come very many diverse Theologies,
And in so doing, we will dilute Scripture."**
John Calvin, in a letter to Phillip Melanchthon Nov 28th, 1552

In this, Calvin was correct.

Calvin is the man that the Presbyterians, Baptists, Congregationalists, and the Reform Church look to as the Spiritual Founder, but you do not follow his Theology. Calvin, like Luther, strongly believed in the Perpetual Virginity of the Blessed Virgin, yet the Faiths that look to him as their Founder do not follow his theology.

The Protestant Faith has often quoted St Paul. Did not St Paul warn against the Protestant Movement?

"I appeal to you my brethren; take note of those who create dissentions in opposition to the Doctrines of the Church, which you have been taught.

Avoid them"
St Paul (Romans) 16:17

Not only has the Protestant Movement created a dissention with the Catholic Church, but even unto itself, with its diversity of Scriptural beliefs. There are NO two Protestant Faiths that have the same theology. Is this not dissention?

Huldrych Zwingali, in 1522 wrote a STRONG defense of the Perpetual Virginity of Mary. Further, he wrote,
"That, to doubt the Perpetual Virginity of Mary is Heresy".

Zwingali added further, that God esteemed Mary above ALL of the Angels and Saints. In Zwingali's last writing, *"Fidel Exposito"* he insisted on the Perpetual Virginity of Mary.

A sermon on "the Perpetual Virginity of Mary" by Zwingali was printed in 1524. In his sermon, Zwingali expounded his faith that Mary was a Perpetual Virgin and to believe otherwise was *dishonorable, unworthy, evil and impious.*

Then we have Heinrich Bullinger. Heinreich Bullinger was the successor to Zwingali, after Zwingali made the fatal mistake of trying to starve out the Catholics in an adjoining Canton (1531).

In 1575, Bullinger defended the Virginity of Mary, stating that *"She is the most Nobel member of the Christian Community."* Further, Bullinger added, that She now lives with Christ in Heaven, as She is Ever Virgin and Mother of God.

Bullinger, along with the German Theologian Johannes Oecolampadius, was a co-author of the Helvetic Confessions, in 1534, which was adopted in 1536. The gist of the Helvetic Confessions was to refute of the theology of Helvidius.

Several hundred years later, **John Wesley** wrote that Jesus was born of a Virgin, and she REMAINED a Pure and Unspotted Virgin throughout Her Life.

Now I ask the followers of Luther, Calvin Zwingali, Wesley, et al, at what point in the time of your churches history, did your Church change its theology? How can the Lutherans, Baptists, Methodists, Presbyterians, et al, claim they are followers of a Founder of the Reformation, and at the same time deny the Founders Theology?

Who, in the "chain of command" of these various religions authorized the refuting of the Founders Theology? If Luther, Calvin, Zwingali, Wesley, et al, are wrong in their theology, why are they not castigated as the Pope and the Catholics are castigated for their belief in the Perpetual Virginity of Mary.

If Luther, Calvin et al, are right in their theology, then why do you Protestants not follow their teachings? You MUST follow their Theology, or denounce them as you do the Catholic Faith. You cannot have it both ways.

Protestants will rail against the Catholic Church for what they believe, that the Catholic Church is teaching false doctrine. Yet here we have some members of the Protestant movement, teaching conflicting theology. Some one has got to be wrong. There is no authority within the Protestant movement to correct a false theology, except if they believe that the false theology comes from the Catholic Church.

Luther, Calvin and Wesley, all believed that "spilling" the seed was immoral. Luther and Calvin both called into account, those that advocated "spilling" the seed. There is absolutely no way around it, Luther and Calvin both condemned birth control. Yet here today, <u>every</u> Protestant Faith, the followers of the Founders of the Reformation, advocating condoms, (birth control).

Luther and Calvin believed that birth control was a sin against God. Life was a miracle from God, and to take means to deny life was an act against God.

Most Protestants will be quick to point out some belief by Catholics, that the Protestant will claim are no where written in Scripture. Sola Scriptura, they claim is the basis for their beliefs. Well here we have, Luther pointing out the Scriptural passage regarding "spilling" the seed as an act against God, but still almost ALL Protestant Faiths endorse artificial mean of birth control. The apology for deviating from Scripture is because it is helps to avoid unwanted pregancies. By avoiding intercourse with some one who is not your wife, would avoid an unwanted pregnancy. It would also avoid millions of abortions. Therefore Protestant advocates the use of condoms, and as a result approve of "spilling" the seed a clear violation of Scripture. So much for Sola Scriptura!

Then we have the acceptance of Mary the Mother of Jesus as a Perpetual Virgin. All three very strongly taught that that Jesus was borne of a Virgin, as Scripture had foretold. Further, they taught that Mary lived and died a Virgin. Their theology further stated that Mary bore no children other than Jesus. Not only has Luther, Calvin, Henry and Wesley proclaimed the Perpetual virginity of Mary, but also Islam teaches like wise.

Martin Luther was very adamant is his belief in the Perpetual Virginity of the Blessed Virgin Mary. Martin Luther proclaimed:

> **"To deny the Perpetual Virginity of Mary,**
> **Is to doubt the Omnipotence of God".**
> Martin Luther

Yet today, the Lutheran Churches deny the Perpetual Virginity of Mary. This is a complete contradiction of their Founder. There are other contradictions.

How many of the Protestant Faiths today, teach that Mary, the mother of Jesus was Immaculate? Just about every Faith that I have studied, has relegated Mary to a mere foot note in Scriptural History, and yet, their Founders proclaimed Mary as Immaculate, and a Perpetual Virgin. They taught that to deny this manifestation, was to deny God.

Protestants are very quick to point out Martin Luther and his 95 thesis castigating the Catholic Church. I found it most interesting, that almost all Protestants only have knowledge of one or two of the complaints of Luther, as documented in his thesis.

What I cannot understand is that Protestants look upon Luther as the George Washington of the Reformation, their Founding Father, but they ignore his Theology. How can this be? Is Luther the Great Theologian who opened the eyes of the masses to the correct Word of God? If so, why is his Theology not being adhered to? If Luther is not this Great Leader, then why is there a Lutheran Church? If the Catholic Church is wrong, then Luther is wrong, because his *core* beliefs coincide with the Theology of Catholicism.

We have but to look at the State of Protestantism today to see what is happening. The Faith that Luther originated has morphed into three separate Theological beliefs. NONE of the three adhere to Luther's Theology. Luther believed in the fundamentals of the Catholic Faith. While he strongly protested the actions of the Pope, he did agree with the core Catholic Theology.

Luther did not accept the concept of Purgatory. Also he took exception to what he interpreted as "paying" for indulgences. Luther was castigated by some of the originators of the Reformation, as being too Catholic in his beliefs.

Luther believed that the Body and Blood of Christ are present in the Holy Eucharist (Communion). At one time, during Services, while distributing Communion, "flakes" of a "Host" fell upon the floor. Luther knelt down and licked the flakes from the floor, so not any would desecrate the Body and Blood of Jesus. Today many in the Protestant Faith look upon Communion as a ritual, in commemoration of the Last Supper, in complete contradiction of the Founder of the Reformation.

Luther believed in the Sacrament of Reconciliation (Confession). Up to the time of his death, Luther participated in "Confession" every week. Reconciliation was a Sacrament of the Lutheran Faith until the late 17th century, a full 200 years after the death of Luther.

There are many differences in Theology being taught today, not only in the Lutheran Faiths, but in other Faiths that claim one of the Founders as the originator of their Faith.

Which modern Lutheran Theologian decided that Luther was wrong? For the Lutheran Church, today, to be right, then Luther is wrong.

You just can not have it both ways.

The Theology, upon which the Lutheran Church and many other Protestant Faiths were founded, is no longer being adhered too.

If the Lutheran Churches no longer follow the Theology of Luther, then why do they call themselves Lutherans? Which Theologian within the Lutheran community had declared the Theology of Luther Passé? Then, if Luther was wrong in his Theology, why is the Lutheran Faith not <u>renamed</u> after this unnamed Theologian?

That also brings up another quandary. Why do the Methodists look upon Wesley as the Founder of their Faith? Wesley had a Theology contrary to the Teachings of the Methodist Church. Wesley was an Anglican Priest. He lived as a Priest and died as an Anglican Priest. He was a very strongly against any deviation from the Anglican Faith. How does the Methodist Faith compare with the Anglican Faith? In my humble belief, they are 180 degrees apart.

While Wesley was not one of the originators of the Reformation, he was, and is, and integral part of the Movement. Basically, he followed the theology of Luther and Calvin. To my knowledge he was not involved in the "inquisition of heretics, as was Luther and Zwingali, but he did marry a widow with four children, and after a few years, did he not abandon her? Could it possibly be because of his "difficult" relations with other women?

John Wesley was an Anglican (Church of England) priest. He practiced his priestly duties throughout his life. He lived and died as an Anglican priest. Others founded the Methodist Faith. The founders of the Methodist Faith took 29 of the 35 articles from the Church of England. Here again, we have the *dilute and destroy* actions of Protestant Faiths.

Not only was the original Methodist Faith a dilution of the Anglican Faith, but the Faith itself, morphed into several other Faiths calling themselves some form or other of the Methodist Beliefs. Each Faith has taken some aspect from the original Faith, and adding, deleting or diluting the original theology.

What were John Wesley's core beliefs? John Wesley believed and taught that Mary, the Mother of Jesus was a Perpetual Virgin. John Wesley was vilified by his contemporaries. They accused him of advocating a reunion with the Catholic Church, because his Core Beliefs were in accordance with Catholicism.

Yet the Faith that looks upon John Wesley as their Cornerstone of Faith, do not adhere to Wesley's own Beliefs and Teachings.

John Wesley's brother Charles had implored John to "stop before he had broken the Bridge" Charles was afraid that the actions of Wesley would "leave an inedible mark on his memory" John assured his brother, that he (John) was and would always be, faithful to the Anglican Faith.

Now here we have a conundrum. A Faith (Methodist) that looks to John Wesley as its founder lived and died as an Anglican Priest. John Wesley believed that Mary, the Mother of Jesus, was a Perpetual Virgin. Is this belief not contrary to core Methodist beliefs?

John Wesley's core Beliefs, parallel that of the Catholic Church to such a degree, that he was accused of seeking reconciliation with Rome.

One aspect of John Wesley's belief that was not in accordance with Rome was his belief in Salvation by "Faith Alone". However he was in accordance with MOST of the Doctrines of Rome, including <u>Apostolic Succession</u>. Where is Apostolic Succession in the Methodist Faith?

Where in the Methodist Faith, is the Veneration of Mary?

Where is the Methodist Church today? Has not that Faith divided, morphed, and united with other Faiths, all of which has "divorced" themselves from the Core theology of John Wesley?

It is a mixed up Theology! Lutherans do not follow the Theology of Martin Luther, and Methodist, who claim John Wesley as their Founder, do not adhere to his theology.

One has to ask "will the real Methodist Church step forward" What was the Methodist Faith immediately after the death of John Wesley, is not the same Faith today. First the Faith has undergone a metamorphoses to a large degree. It has ebbed and flowed with the changing whims of modern day society, unlike another Faith that has maintained the same Theology since the time of Christ. In my humble opinion, the Methodist Church has discarded some Beliefs and added new ones, which are contrary to Scripture. The Methodist Church is nowhere near the Beliefs of John Wesley. John Wesley, before his death, <u>implored his followers to remain in the Anglican Faith</u>.

. Nondenominational Faiths are springing up like weeds in the Garden of God. Did not Our Lord say that at the Last Day, the Weeds will be separated from the Wheat, and thrown into Eternal Fire?

Protestant Faiths are built upon a foundation of Sand, ever changing, ever shifting. Did not Our Lord build His church upon a Rock? A Rock that is solid and inviolate. A Rock that withstands the forces of those who oppose it, unlike the Sand, that gives way, and changes with Time.

Our Lord had said that He would be with His Church until the Last Day. I would ask my Protestant friends,

"When did Our Lord leave the Catholic Church, and accept your Church?

All Protestant Faiths are teaching a Theology contrary to the Theology of all the Founders of the Reformation There is not ONE single Protestant Faith today, which has not morphed, changed, revised, amended and or compromised on the Original Theology of the Reformation. If the Originators of the Reformation were right, then those who have deviated from their teaching are wrong. If the Originators of the Reformation were wrong, then Protestantism is wrong.

There was a cartoon in the comic pages of the Chicago Tribune on June 23rd, 2006, which, in reality demonstrates (to me) more truth than fiction. In the cartoon, a group of Protestant Ministers are debating on how they could revive their dwindling congregations. One of the Ministers suggests that perhaps it would help increase membership, if instead of 10 Commandments, that they would go with 5 commandments instead.

Many a Truth is Spoken in Jest!

Since all Protestant Faiths teach a contrary Theology, I would ask the One True Protestant Faith come forward and declare itself.

So far NONE has.

15

Sins of the Founders of the Reformation

All my life I have heard of the Catholic Church and the sins of the Spanish Inquisition. One would get the idea that this was like Chicago's Warren Boulevard, only ONE Way. However with a very little effort, one can find that this event in history was multifaceted. Not only did the Catholics execute so called heretics, but also the Moslems <u>and the Protestants</u>.

In having discourse with Protestants, they ALWAYS bring up the "sins" of the Catholic Church. None of them seems to know of any of the "sins" of the Founding Fathers of the Reformation and their agents.

Now I fully realize that two wrongs do not make a right, but by suppressing the "sins" of the Protestant Founders, one cannot get a complete understanding of their Faith, and gives the illusion of a "sinless" faith. Catholics, Protestants, and Moslems need to inform their flock and potential converts of their sins along with their tenets, Jesus of Nazareth Church International, recommends that Pastors admit to their "sins" to their congregation at least once a year.

It seems that everyone knows of the "sins" of the Catholic church and its Popes, but what of Luther, Calvin Zwingali et al? What of the Protestant inquisition and the abuse by Protestant clergy?

MARTIN LUTHER

When it comes to blaming the Pope and Catholics for the deaths of many accused of heresy, Luther stands there with "unclean hands". By claiming that Suleiman was the "Wrath of God sent to punish the Catholics", Luther encouraged the Germans to refrain from coming to the aid of Hungary, As we said earlier, 10's of thousand of Catholics were slaughtered in a few hours time at the Battle of Mohacs. Only because of the resistance of a lone Austrian Castle, off the invasion route, that refused to surrender, was Vienna saved. Suleiman's vanity would not accept defiance of his offer of generous terms. Still the Austrians resisted, and as a result were overwhelmed and slaughtered, men, women and children. The resistance allowed Luther time to change his mind and declare Suleiman the enemy of God and must be resisted.

But then, what of the German peasants?

The peasants were encouraged by Martin Luther's Treatise,

"Freedom of the Christian Man".

Thinking that Luther's writing advocated their freedom, the peasants demanded their freedom from serfdom. However it appears that Luther was beholden to the German Nobility.

Did he not issue a license to the Landgrave of Hesse, to have two wives? Also, did not Luther side with the German Nobility, in order to regain some of the property that the German Nobility confiscated from the Catholic Church?

In coming out against the peasants, Luther wrote a Treatise,

"*Against the Murderous Peasants*".

He further advised the Nobility that it was Just and Lawful to kill the peasants

"*as one would kill a mad dog*".

Further, Luther advised that

"a Prince may more easily gain Heaven

by shedding the Blood of the Rebel Serf, that others do by praying."

As a result of Luther's approval, the Nobility suppressed the Revolt. Thousands of Serfs were hung from trees along the route of their retreat. The leaders of the revolt were horribly tortured and suffered a very slow and extremely painful death. In all, well over **100,000 peasants** were executed. As a result of this episode in Luther's history, he earned the title of *"Dr Liar"*, by the German peasants.

How many of you know of Luther's publications regarding the defaming of Jews. Luther had published a pamphlet in 1543, shortly before his death, *"The Jews and Their Lies"*. This tract could have been written by *Adolph Hitler*. It very well could have been what Hitler used as his blue print for the Holocaust. Luther had the Jews expelled from his home State of Saxony. These are just some of the actions of the greatest (saintly?) Reformer.

Huldrych Zwingali

Here we have another of the Founders of the Reformation. In 1522 Zwingali called the Bible the "sole" source of Faith. As such he abolished the Sacraments of Penance (Reconciliation) and Extreme Unction (anointing of the Sick). He ordered all pictures, statues and relics of Saints removed from his Church. The order also included Alters and the organs. I, for one, cannot imagine a Protestant service without some kind of music.

But then, what of Zwingali the man of God? It is an historical fact that he led a very immoral life. On many occasions he had "pleasures of the flesh". Zwingali is known to have cohabitated with Anne Richards. He later married her, to "make an honest woman of her".

Zwingali not only had recourse against the Catholics, but had a great enmity regarding Anabaptists. They along with Catholics were persecuted mercilessly. Imprisonment, torture and death were common.

Some Catholics and Anabaptists were "lucky" to only suffer exile. The normal final penalty, under Zwingali was, drowning, burning at the Stake, and sometimes beheading. Zwingali proclaimed that the "Anabaptists should be sought out wherever they are and should be drowned, and NONE should be spared."

Perhaps the reason that Zwingali has been relegated to the lower echelon of Protestantism is that he made a serious mistake in attempting to subdue Catholicism in the Swiss Canton adjoining his. Zwingali provoked the conflict by cutting of the food supplies to the Catholics. His Army left Zurich and advanced on the Catholics. On October 11th, 1531, at the battle of Kappel, Zwingali's army was defeated and Zwingali was slain.

While Zwingali had differed with Luther on many facets of theology, he did strongly agree with Luther on *the "Perpetual Virginity of Mary"*.

Anabaptist did not believe in infant Baptism, and as such, re baptized the adults who joined their Faith. This appears to be something that modern day Protestants subscribes to.

John Calvin

John Calvin followed the same vein as Luther and Zwingali regarding the punishment of "unbelievers" (heretics). In the Constitution of Geneva, the Death Penalty was decreed for:
- Witchcraft
- Blasphemy
- Heresy

In a very short span of time, 58 sentences of Death were imposed. Even more were exiled from Geneva.

Calvin took personal revenge upon two of his "critics". Servetus opposed Calvin's theology, and as such angered Calvin. Servetus was invited to come to Geneva and discuss this matter with Calvin. When Servetus arrived he was arrested and sentenced to death by burning at the Stake. Normally, death occurs within five minutes in "burning at the Stake" However, in the case of Servetus, green wood was used, and Servetus suffered for almost 30 minutes before he expired.

James Gruet posted a note which called for Calvin to leave the city of Geneva. Upon hearing of this, Calvin had Gruet arrested, and an extensive search was conducted for any accomplices, or any evidence of heresy or blasphemy. All that was found was one of Calvin's religious Tracts, upon which Gruet is "alleged" to have written"

"Rubbish"

Gruet was put on the "Rack" twice a day, morning and evening" for an entire month. Gruet would not recant, and as such, was sentenced to death for blasphemy. Gruet was beheaded on July 26th, 1547. Gruet was one of many heretics that died due to John Calvin's reign of Religious rule of Geneva.

As to the cruel inhuman execution of Servetus, Calvin replied to his critics by writing a tract *"Against the Errors of Servetus"* in 1544. In his treatise, Calvin declared that he was indifferent to the accusations (of his enemies) of cruelty. Further, he reiterated that he would gladly do again, what he had done to Servetus Not only was he happy, but he *"spits in the face of his detractors"*.

Henry III.

Now we come to a man who is somewhat of a paradox. Very many know of Henry regarding his 6 wives. On the other side of the "coin" few really know of his Theological Beliefs. Yet, because of Henry, the break with the Catholic Church, and the Founding of the Church of England (Anglican/Episcopal Church) Faith was born. Unlike the other Protestants that were to follow Luther and Henry, the Catholic Church did not compromise its Theology to accommodate an element of society. Henry would have stayed a Catholic, if the Pope had granted him a divorce from Queen Katherine. Henry wanted a son, and Katherine was unable to accommodate him.

Katherine produced a daughter, Mary, who would eventually become Queen of England. Queen Mary, lived and died, trying to return England to the Catholic Faith.

Anne Boleyn, his second wife, produced another daughter, Elizabeth, who would eventually ascend the Throne of England as Elizabeth I.

The irony of history is that Elizabeth I was instrumental in founding of the British Empire and Elizabeth II is instrumental in disbanding the British Empire.

Queen Mary had spared Elizabeth's life when she was led to believe that Elizabeth would renounce the Anglican Faith and reaffirm the Faith of Rome.

Jane Seymour would give Henry the son he desired, but at the cost of Jane's life. The irony of it all is that the son Henry wanted, so as to perpetuate his lineage, was to die before his 17th birthday, never begetting an offspring. The Throne of England went to a woman. Henry gave up his Faith, all for naught.

Henry's fourth wife, he abandoned (divorced) very shortly after the wedding.

His fifth wife Catherine Howard was a victim of a plot to discredit her, because the plotters believed that she would lead Henry back to the Catholic Church.

Henry's sixth and last wife Katherine Parr, not only outlived Henry, but also 3 of her 4 husbands. There was no heir to the Throne from the last 3 wives of Henry. Here we have a vain King, defying Rome regarding the sanctity of marriage, so that he could gain a male heir, who would rule England in his place. And all for naught.

As result of Henry's vanity the Church of England was born. Today it is known as the Anglican/ Episcopalian Church. The Anglican/Episcopalian Church has as its leader, the Arch Bishop of Canterbury, Rowan Williams. Though I wonder just what authority he does have. We have touched on this earlier.

In Christendom, other than the Orthodox Faiths, the Anglican/Episcopalian Faith is "close" to the Catholic Beliefs.

What of Henry the "Inquisitor"

In my personal opinion Henry formatted the Blue print for persecution of those who opposed his Rule. Lands were confiscated from "unbelievers". Many were driven from their homes. Many, very many were executed.

Henry, like Adolph Hitler, who I believe used Henry's Blue print to try to destroy the Jews, used surrogates to fulfill his Pogrom. Hitler used his lackeys, like Adolph Eichmann, Heinrich Himmler, Reinhardt Heydrich and Joseph Mengele, just to name a few.

With Henry, it was Thomas Cromwell, Thomas Cranmer, Hugh Latimer and John Knox, just to name a few.

Thomas Cromwell

Now Thomas Cromwell is not to be confused with Oliver Cromwell of later infamy. Oliver came much later, but was just as deadly to those of the Catholic Faith as was Thomas.

Thomas Cromwell was the King's Vicar General, and as such had authority over the Arch Bishop, Just as today, the Queen has power over the Arch Bishop. Here was the inception of the practice of *the State ruling the Church*, making the Arch Bishop (in a sense) a puppet. It was Thomas Cromwell who in 1530 brought about many of the changes for the Church of England (Anglican).

> Royal Supremacy of the State over the Church
> Printing the Bible in English
> Had Monasteries closed
> Ordered the destruction of Shrines
> Abolished *some* Holy Days

The methods used by Thomas Cromwell, was worthy of Hitler or Stalin. It was a system of fear, torture, and execution. Stalin did use exile to some dissidents. The exile Stalin enforced was exile to Siberia, which was in reality, a living death.

Those who criticized his divorce from Katherine of Aragon, or those denying the Supremacy of Henry over the Church of Rome, were accused of Treason. Under Thomas Cromwell's law, those executed were not Christian martyrs, but enemies of the STATE.

What was the punishment for (Catholics) High Treason? It was *disembowelment while still alive*. Hanging and quartering, also was another form of punishment for those who were defending their Catholic Faith.

Thomas Cromwell was a genius, albeit an evil one, in creating the "Double Grand Jury". The Grand Jury would hear the evidence and declare the defendant either guilty or that there was insufficient evidence to prosecute, If the verdict was Guilty, then the defendant was brought to trial and the outcome was a foregone conclusion.

Should the Grand Jury find that there was insufficient evidence, the defendant was released (for the time being). But then a second Grand Jury was impaneled. The second Grand Jury would hear evidence against the First Grand Jury. The Charge was malfeasance, and, as being an enemy of the State. If the members of the First Grand Jury were found Guilty, and almost ALL of them were, they would suffer the fate that would have been imposed upon the original defendants. As you can surmise, very, very few defendants were found Not Guilty by the First Grand Jury, as a result of the threat of the Second Grand Jury. The threat of the Second Grand Jury was enough to insure a "correct" verdict (Guilty) by the First Grand Jury.

But then Thomas Cromwell, on behalf of Henry, was an even more (evil) genius. In order to speed the enforcement of the Establishment of the Church of England, Thomas Cromwell came up with the *Act of Attainder*. This was an Act that allowed the execution of enemies of the State without benefit of Trial. Among the victims of this diabolic Act, was the Saintly Sir Thomas More.

Sir Thomas More had been a life long friendship with Henry. At that time, Henry was still a Catholic. Henry depended a great deal on Sir Thomas More for political, economic and religious advice.

On behalf of Henry, (before his break with Rome) and in Henry's name, Sir Thomas More wrote a rebuttal to Martin Luther. The rebuttal that Thomas wrote and Henry approved is entitled *"A defense of the Seven Sacraments"*. This was a severe repudiation of Luther for his break with Rome, and much before Henry's own Schism.

When Thomas More refused to sign the *"Act of Succession"*, and would not take an "Oath of Supremacy" Cromwell had Thomas executed on July 7th, 1535. Before Thomas More was beheaded, he gave a message that should be heeded today. Thomas More said

"I was the King's Good Servant, but God's First.
This message is something we should all adhere to.
God and Country, not Country and God.

Besides Thomas More, there were many others including Bishop Fisher, and many Monks and Friars. All were victims of Thomas Cromwell and the *Act of Attainder*. All the others were disemboweled, while still alive. I wonder how many Catholics or Protestants of today would accept that fate, rather than renounce their Faith? Thomas Cromwell was rewarded with many lands and estates, including the Lewes Priory, which had been Catholic Church property. Also included were Church property in Colchester, St Osith and Launde.

Thomas Cromwell finally became a victim of his own Law. Under the Act of Attainder, Cromwell was caused to be executed by his jealous enemies at Court.

Arch Bishop Cranmer

Thomas Cranmer, Arch Bishop of Canterbury, wrote many fine words, including the English Prayer Book, and yet he had a dark side. It did not compare with Henry and Cromwell, but never the less his story is far from "Saintly". While Cranmer did have a "dark" side, it did not compare with his two contemporaries.

Cranmer came to power through Anne Boleyn. He wrote the opinion that favored the divorce of Henry from Katherine of Aragon. Through Anne's patronage, Henry appointed Cranmer the First Arch Bishop of Canterbury. Cranmer, despite being under the "Vow of Celibacy", had a German wife that he kept secluded.

Arch Bishop Cranmer presided over the executions of not only Catholics, but also Protestant detractors. Many Protestant extremists were executed for holding the same Theological views as Cranmer, but Cranmer held his views secret until he thought it was safe to disagree with the King. Arch Bishop Cranmer officiated at the marriage of Henry to Anne Boleyn. Three years later, when Anne was accused of adultery, Cranmer turned against her, and ordered her execution. Before the execution, Cranmer tried to have the marriage of Anne to Henry declared invalid. This was an effort to remove Elizabeth from the line of Succession.

Here Cranmer created a dilemma. Among those accused was the brother of Anne. They were also tried, as having committed incest. Now, if the marriage to Henry was declared invalid, then there could be no charge of adultery.

There were four others who were condemned along with Anne and her brother. The usual punishment for incest was burning at the stake, and for adultery, it was to be hanged, and then cut down before the individual expired, and while still alive, were *drawn and quartered*, a most painful death. However the sentences for all, was commuted to beheading.

Henry had not been satisfied with the attempt to declare his marriage to Anne invalid, as he was most desirous to have Jane Seymour as his new bride, so Henry completed the *order of execution* of Anne and those accused with her.

Cranmer also oversaw the destruction and or confiscation of numerous Catholic Church properties. Very many priests, Nuns and laity were executed. Among those accused was Friar Forrest. On April 8th, 1538, Friar Forrest was taken to Lambeth.

Cranmer demanded that Friar Forrest denounce the Pope and proclaim Henry as the legitimate Head of the Church. This Friar Forrest refused to do. He was then taken to Smithfield and burned at the stake.

I wonder today, how many "Christians" would defend their Faith at the risk of a horrible death.

In 1540, Arch Bishop Cranmer was caught in an impending dilemma. The aging King was leaning toward a more liberal attitude regarding Catholics. So Cranmer expanded the "Reign of Terror" to include many Protestants. But when the aging King took as his fifth wife, 20 year old Kathryn Howard, Cranmer feared that Kathryn would lead Henry back to the Catholic Church. Cranmer orchestrated a campaign to discredit Kathryn. Kathryn was accused of fornication before her marriage to Henry and adultery after her marriage to Henry.

Cranmer personally over saw the interrogation (torture) of those accused of carnal relations with Kathryn. As a result, Cranmer's verdict was that Kathryn and her (accused) lovers were executed.

Kathryn could have escaped the death sentence if she would admit to the charges against her. Had she admitted to them, she would have suffered the punishment of being exiled. However she would not admit to the false charges against her, so she valiantly went to her death.

When Henry died, Arch Bishop Cranmer assumed a favorable position on the *Council of Regency*. This was supposed to be for the protection of the boy King, Edward VI. Cranmer allied himself with the Duke of Suffolk and the "Lord Protector" Somerset. Cranmer was now free to exploit his true agenda, and began plundering more Catholic Church properties.

When Somerset was removed, in a coup orchestrated by the Duke of Northumberland, John Dudley, Cranmer again showed his true colors by signing the Death Warrant on Somerset.

Now allied with Dudley, Catholic churches were stripped of silver and gold. Books were burned in huge bonfires. Despite being the First Signatory of King Henry's Will, which guaranteed the Succession of Mary and Elizabeth, Arch Bishop Cranmer violated his Oath and backed an attempt to place Lady Jane Grey on the Throne. Lady Jane Grey was Queen of England for only 9 days.

This was a desperate Act of Treason, and as a result Arch Bishop Cranmer was condemned to death.

With Queen Mary (a Catholic) the daughter of Catherine of Aragon upon the Throne of England, Cranmer attempted to save his life by denouncing his Protestant beliefs. This was just another flip flop by Cranmer.

Cranmer was for Anne Boleyn, and then turned against her.

Cranmer was for sanctioning the marriage of Anne to Henry, and then he wanted to invalidate the marriage.

He was for Summerset, and then turned against him.

He portrayed himself as loyal to Henry, and then violated his duty to the late King, for his own personal quest for power.

He portrayed himself as a life long Protestant, and then tried to save himself from execution by denouncing his Protestant Faith, and tried to embrace Catholicism. All to no avail.

Perhaps it was Cranmer's history of flipping flopping that was instrumental in causing a cancelling a conference between himself, Calvin, Bullinger (Zwingali's successor) and Melanchthon (Luther's successor). The purpose of the conference was an attempt to unite ALL Protestant Faiths.

The Protestant faction was against convening with the "Church of England" as Henry had castigated the Protestants for removal of five of the Sacraments from Holy Scripture. They in turn had castigated Henry as a Polygamist, as they recognized Henry's divorces as a violation of Scripture.

Through all of Henry's 6 marriages, he had two divorces, two executions, one died in childbirth, and one outlived him. The son he longed for suffered a mysterious death before his maturity.

The people that Henry had placed in a position of authority

had used their power for their own gratification. The end result was that most of those he placed in power, suffered the same fate that they had decreed on their victims, execution, plus Henry was denied the male heir to ascend the Throne of England. That was the original reason for his divorce from Katherine.

Perhaps the greatest paradox of Henry's Church, is that, up to today, the Church had looked upon divorce as against God's Law. Edward the VIII had to give up his right to the Throne, on December 12 1936 because he, as *De Jure* Head of the Church of England would be violating the Church of England's Theology, which forbade remarriage after a divorce.

What a change has taken place within the Church of England. Adapt with the times it appears. Charles, the future *De Jure* Head of the Church of England, has lived in an openly adulterous relationship, so the Church, rather than perform a wedding, instead "blessed": his union.

This action is but a continuation of all Protestant Faiths.ABdilute and destroy, and accommodate the whims of the most vocal. Charles has indicated that when he is King, one of his titles would be <u>"Defender of the Faith"</u>.

One can readily see the dilemma that is growing within the Anglican/Episcopal Faith. One faction teaches that the Homosexual act is a sin, and another faction says it is compatible with Christian Doctrine, and have already ordained homosexual priests and bishops.

Since Charles has already defended his adulterous relationship, he most probably will defend the acceptance of homosexuality and the blessings of their unions, when he becomes *De Jure*, Head of the Anglican Community.

Already, the Church of England is on the verge of a Schism, while the *de facto* Head of the Church, Arch Bishop Rowan Williams, who appears to be a man with no authority, or if he has, like former President Buchannan, rings his hands and asks for "time" to look into this matter,

I for one cannot see a Catholic Pope standing idly by and doing nothing, as the Church is being torn apart. When Arch Bishop Marcel Lefebvre defied the Pope, by not accepting the ruling by Vatican II, and by consecrating Bishops, in defiance of the Pope, he was excommunicated.

Arch Bishop Rowan Williams is standing on a Theological pivotal point in the History of Christendom. What he does, or does not do, will not only affect the Anglican Community, but Protestantism as a whole. The choice Arch Bishop Rowan Williams has is to be like President Abraham Lincoln, and take decisive steps to preserve the Union (Church), or like President Buchannan, be indecisive and watch the fragmentation of the (Union) Anglican Community.

This is a very tough dilemma for a man who appears to be only a "figure head" leader. *Dilute and destroy,* that is the result of an organization with no real leader and no Central Authority, a phenomenon that has prevailed throughout the Protestant movement from the time of Luther and Calvin.

Arch Bishop Rowan Williams, stands on the brink of history. He will either be known as the man who preserved the Anglican Community, of was an unwitting instrument of its fragmentation, a <u>Schism, within a Schism.</u>

HUGH LATIMER

Hugh Latimer was a close associate of Arch Bishop Cranmer and as such rose to the rank of Bishop of London. While Latimer is referred to as a "Saintly Martyr", he was involved with the burning of Franciscans and Anabaptists. He was also involved with the death of Friar John Forrest. Arch Bishop Cranmer complained that Latimer was lax in his treatment of Forrest at Newgate prison, Latimer, then had Forrest chained across a Holy Statue from the church of Lianderfel in Wales, and had him burned alive.

Also, in 1548, with the "boy King" in power (?), Latimer presided over the heresy trials. Latimer went along with Cranmer in justifying the execution of Lord Seymour. Then in 1549, he was instrumental in accusing Joan of Kent of heresy, and then in condemning her to death. Joan of Kent (Joan Bocher) was burned at the stake on May 2, 1550.

The boy King had at first refused to sign the order of execution, but Latimer persuaded him to sign the order of execution.

Under Queen Mary, who ascended the Throne of England, with the mysterious death of the boy King, Cranmer, Ridley and Latimer all suffered the same fate that they had decreed on THOUSANDS of Catholics.

JOHN KNOX

John Knox was a follower of Calvin. On May 29, 1546 Knox gave approval for the murder of the Catholic Cardinal David Beaton at St Andrews. In his (Knox) writings, he stated his views that any Protestant had the right to slaughter any Catholic, whenever they had the opportunity.

Under Knox, an unofficial Parliament was set up, and it decreed death to all Catholics. When an attempt was made on the life of Queen Mary, a Catholic, and the plotters had only killed her Counselor, Knox had two statements to make.

First he said the act (the attempted assassination) "was worthy of all praise". The second, being "Foolish Scotland hath disobeyed God, by sparing the Queen". This Holy (?) writ was from the man who is noted as the Founder of the Presbyterian Faith.

As bad as this was, it did not compare with any of his contemporaries. .

16

MARTIN LUTHER
SAINT OR SINNER, HERO OR ROGUE

Is Martin Luther, the "hero" of the Reformation, or was he one who betrayed the very people who looked to him for Salvation and Freedom? There are those that say that Luther was a Monarchist and used the Monarchy to his advantage. Zwingali was a Republican and was opposed to Luther's alliance with Royalty. The question is, did Luther use the Monarchy to his personal advantage, or did the Monarchy use Luther as their pawn?

What is known at the time is that the Monarchy gave Luther refuge against the Pope. Some will say that this was in retaliation against the Pope not naming a German as the Head of the Holy Roman Empire. Whether Luther sought out the Germans, or the Germans sought out Luther is irrelevant. What is known is the *result*, in that the German Nobility profited greatly from the Reformation, in acquiring vast amount of Catholic Church properties. Some of the property was returned to the Lutheran Church. Luther made it possible for the Government to control the Church, instead of the Church dictating to the National Government, or at the very least, being independent.

Another question would be, did Luther promise the Nobility Church property in return for their assistance in combating the Pope, or did the Nobility demand Church property as a reward to aiding Luther? Either way, the result was the same. Luther got protection, and the Nobility got vast amounts of Church property, property that Luther did not own. Little did Luther or any historian know at that time, that a similar financial maneuver would be used to help defeat (Nazi) Germany, four centuries later.

In 1941, England was in dire straights, and on the verge of being starved out, by German U-Boats. The United States had a Neutrality Act, which forbade us to "give" financial or material assistance to ANY party engaged in a War.

The United States "circumvented" the Law by "lending" the material, and food stuffs. In exchange, Britain Leased Bases to the United States. We lent them material and they leased us Bases. Quid Pro Quo.

Britain desperately needed Destroyers to protect their convoys bringing food and material to England. Britain did not have enough destroyers and the USA had well over 50 "Moth Balled" destroyers available, but the Neutrality forbade us from "giving" the ships to Britain.

Henry Morgenthau, Secretary of the Treasury, took a page out of Luther's "financial" maneuvers, regarding paying German Nobility with Catholic Church property which Luther did not own. Morgenthau proposed that the British "pay" for the destroyers with the Gold that the Vichy French held on the Island of Martinique in the Caribbean. Morgenthau further stated that it was not necessary for Britain to invade Martinique. The Gold was there, and the French could not move it out of Martinique, and after the War, it would be the property of Britain and then the "physical" transfer could be made. In the meantime, it was only necessary to make a "paper" transfer.

Henry Morgenthau was a Jew born in Germany. He was avid in financial affairs and evidently learned well, for the lesson he learned from medieval History helped to bring about the downfall of the Nazi (German) regime.

The German peasants looked to Luther as their *succor*, one who would deliver them from the tyranny of the German Nobility.

You all know what the results were. *Don't you?* This episode in Luther's history is not readily available to most Protestants, much less those that call themselves Lutherans. Yet the *history* is there

My personal opinion is that the Germans used Luther, not as a hero, but to their own advantage. Was Luther a villain? You should ask the widows of the peasants who were killed in the Uprising. This was an "uprising" against tyranny of the German Nobility. This was an Uprising in which the peasants took Luther at his Word regarding Freedom. After all, did not Luther say that "any plowman can interpret Scripture"? Therefore the peasants took Luther's admonition to heart, and believed that he would support them against the German Nobility as he said he would against the Pope.

The peasants did not realize that the "freedom" that Luther railed about, was freedom from the rules set by the Pope, not freedom from tyranny of the German Nobility.

Most every ardent Protestant, with whom I have a religious discourse, will quote me chapter and verse regarding the "alleged" machinations of most any Pope. But then, when there is a mention of similar machinations by not only Luther, but also other of the Founders of the Reformation, they will vehemently deny any such event had occurred. I find it most interesting, and yet disconcerting, that the very same people that will accuse some Pope of "irregularities", will take umbrage with me and accuse me of denigrating the memory of a "Saint".

A Saint? Well let us take another look at "saint" Martin. Luther had an antagonistic relationship with the Pope. Part of what Luther had rebelled against, regarding the Pope, was within reason. Those impediments were very long ago resolved. Luther believed strongly in very many Core Beliefs of the Catholic Church.

Now before you begin to rail against me and vent your spleen, stop and analyze the Theology of Martin Luther and how it may differ from your Beliefs. I can tell you what Luther believed <u>Theologically,</u> and is recorded in history. I will state categorically that today's Lutherans, and almost ALL Protestant

Theology is 180 degrees from the Theology of not only Luther, but ALL the Founding Fathers of the Reformation.

We said it before, and we will say it again, that maybe it is time for you to examine your conscience. Exam your Theology, and compare it with the Theology of the Founders of the Birth of Protestantism.

Ask yourselves:

Do you believe in Transubstantiation? That being that the Body and Blood of Our Savior is present in the Holy Eucharist.
Martin did so believe.

Do you believe in the Perpetual Virginity of the Blessed Virgin, the mother of Jesus?
Martin Luther did so believe, as did Calvin and Zwingali.

Do you believe that Mary, the mother of Jesus, had other offspring?
Martin Luther said to believe that, was to denigrate the Divinity of Jesus.

Do you believe in Divorce?
Luther, Calvin and Zwingali all vilified Henry VIII as a polygamist, and none of them sanctioned divorce.

Do you believe in infant Baptism?
Martin Luther did.

Do you believe in Birth Control?
Martin Luther and the other Founders of the Reformation held that "to spill the seed outside the vagina was an abomination (sin).

Do you believe in a homosexual life style?
This is against the teachings of the Founders of the Reformation.

It appears to me that the Founders of the Reformation firmly believed if the Core Theology of the Catholic Church. Their major objection of Catholicism was the Pope. This, to me, is the ONLY belief universally followed by Protestants today.

It has been my experience, that all of the Core Beliefs held by Martin Luther are today contrary to the Beliefs of almost every Protestant Faith. This is somewhat of an enigma.

Perhaps, some day, a Lutheran, or any other Protestant, who looks to Luther as the Founder of the Reformation, will explain to me how they can look upon Luther as a great Theologian, and yet abandon his Theology. To me, it comes down to either Luther was right and today you are following a false doctrine, or you are right and Luther, et al, were heretics.

The philosophy of the Protestants seems to be:
I believe in the Teachings of Our Lord Jesus Christ, <u>EXCEPT</u>, etc, etc, etc.

Each and every Protestant denomination has a Theology of its own. Taking some of Our Lord's Teachings and ignoring some and denying others. Since the middle of the 16th Century, the Protestant Reformation has been in a state of flux. Some have morphed, some have fragmented, and some have ceased to exist. Still others have joined together, accepting some of the Teachings of each group and modifying others to accommodate the union of two diverse Theologies.

Not one single Protestant Faith today has the same Theology expounded by the Founders of the Reformation, Luther, Calvin, Zwingali, and of course Henry VIII.

Luther, Calvin and Zwingali all believed that there had to be ONE Faith. Failure to achieve that, it would then be better to return to Catholicism. Even Henry, in his last days, harbored the thought of returning to the Catholic Faith. But the plot to discredit Kathryn Howard ended that possibility. Luther had thought that with his leadership every one would join him in his battle against the Pope. In this he was sadly mistaken.

The Anglican, Orthodox, and Lutheran Faiths have all, at one time or another sought reconciliation with the Holy See. The One Major doctrine that these various Faiths could not accept is the Supremacy of the Pope.

Calvin warned Melanchthon that failure to unify would spawn a plethora of various and contradictory "Christian" beliefs that in the end would dilute and weaken Christianity.

Melanchthon could not accept Calvin's Theology of Predestination, and therefore made a futile attempt to bring the follower of Luther back to the Catholic Church.

You who have eyes to see and ears to hear should be able to see and hear what is transpiring in the world today. The public display of Christianity is being thwarted, in that a display of a crèche in any facility related to the Government is forbidden. This also includes public schools where children may no longer sing Christmas carols, as that would be an endorsement of a religion by the State.

It is all well and good, for the American Civil Liberties Union (ACLU) to say they are not suppressing religion, but defending the Constitution, which they allege (wrongly), mandates the separation of Church and State. Here again, they use the same axiom employed by the Protestants in their interpretation of Scripture, which is, taking articles out of context, and assuming others that are not in evidence.

ACLU claims that it is not suppressing Christianity, but merely prohibiting Christianity from using Government facilities for evangelization. Overtly and I believe covertly ACLU is encouraging individuals and groups to bring suit against any Christian display, or any word, deed or sign relating to Christianity, and have them removed from any display that is in slightest related to government.

ACLU, to me, is aiding and abetting in suits to remove the phrase "under God" from the pledge of Allegiance, and also to have the Motto "In God we Trust" removed from our currency. It will not be too much longer, before a suit will be brought to remove any tax exemption for any and ALL Christian Churches, including removing the tax exemption for individuals who contribute to Churches and contributions to "Christian" charities.

The fragmentation of Protestant Faiths has so weakened the interpretation of Scripture, that today, the interpretation of Marriage is threatened and the Homosexual Life Style is being accepted as approved in Scripture. ACLU has taken advantage of the divisions within Protestantism, to overtly or covertly encourage individual groups to bring suit to attack the Sanctity of Marriage and the approval of Homosexual Unions.

Many Nondenominational Faiths, succumbing to "political" pressure, and attempting to gain new converts, are now accepting a Homosexual Life Style as being "Christian". No where, in Scripture, does it allow for Homosexuality, but it definitely does forbid the Act of;

"A *Man lying with a Man, as with a Woman is an Abomination* (Sin)"

Where does an individual or group acquire the funds to bring Suit against Christian Beliefs? The costs in bringing about these various Suits, is astronomical, and the average person or group does not have their own resources to fund these legal filings. It is my belief, that they get the funds and lawyers from ACLU. And where does ACLU get their funds? You utilize the axiom "follow the money". A great deal of funds do come from anti religious groups, but as far as I can find out, the VAST majority of the funding for these various anti Christian suits are funds from the Government. A quirk in the Law allows for compensation to those individuals (ACLU) who are contesting a Law pertaining to separation of Church and State. From what I have deduced, ACLU has been compensated many millions of dollars for aiding and assisting challenges in Court for anti religious individual and groups.

One would think that due to the magnitude of Luther's actions in defying the Pope, and establishing a new Faith, that he, (Luther) would have been instructed by a physical sign from God.

Sola Scriptura. When Martin Luther was questioned about his interpretation of Scripture, Luther replied "that any plowman can interpret the Bible". There is NO reference in Scripture to this Belief.

The plethora of Protestant Faiths that have spawned since 1520, give credence to what I personally believe as a very Foolish, if not Stupid Statement. The proof is in the many contrary interpretations of Scripture by Protestant Faiths.

One Faith says Yes, another says No, and still another says Right, and then another will say Wrong. One says Black, and still another says White, etc, etc, etc, and into infinity. The various contradictory Theologies of the plethora of Protestant Faiths belie the validity of Protestantism.

The kindest word one can give regarding Luther's statement is that he was misguided. My personal interpretation is that it was an arrogant, stupid act of defiance of Papal Authority. Add to that fact is that the statement, by Luther was, and is contrary to Scripture (Parable of the Sown Seeds).

Luther's pronouncement is tantamount to the Founding Fathers of the United States saying "any farmer can interpret the Constitution". How ludicrous that would be! Just imagine the legal mess we would have here in the United States. It would be legal chaos and anarchy. This is indeed the State of Protestantism today. The ONLY issue that binds them together is Anti Catholicism.

Just explore the legal system here in the USA. An issue is brought before the Court and a Verdict is rendered. Then the loser goes to the Appeals Court. Here again the matter is resolved, sometime upholding the lower Court, and sometime overturning the Lower Court.

Once again the matter is brought before the District Court, and finally before the Supreme Court. Then at the Supreme Court, there are nine Justices (Judges) who will study the matter for months at a time. It is very rare that there is a Unanimous decision by the nine Justices. More often than not, the Justices will render a decision by a 5 to 4 vote

There is no way in "hell" that everyone can understand and interpret the Constitution. We know how "we would like it to be". But what we believe and what we want as LEGAL are most often then not, not what we thought.

"If every plowman" can interpret Scripture, then way are there so many different interpretations? The Protestants "claim" that they are guided by the Holy Spirit.

How can the Holy Spirit render so many contradictory interpretations?

Did not Our Lord say "One Fold, One Shepherd". If there is to be of One Fold and One Shepherd, then there **MUST be ONE SCRIPTURE**.

From the very beginning, Luther had hoped to bring about a Change in the Catholic Church. When the Catholic Church would not Change, Luther was caught in a dilemma, because Scripture mandates that people must submit to authority. With this dilemma, Luther then proclaimed the Supremacy of the Scripture. Scripture was to be the Authority.

Here in the USA, the Constitution is the Authority. How many of you would love to have the "right" to interpret the Constitution as YOU saw fit? You don't like a law or rule; you interpret it the way YOU believe it should be. This would be an open invitation to chaos.

One has but to look at what history has recorded, regarding Luther's alliance with German Nobility. With the protection of the German Nobility, Luther was able to Found his Reformation Movement. German Nobility was rewarded with much of the Catholic Church property, a small price for Luther to pay, as he did not own the property.

The irony of the early stages of the Reformation is that there was a very strong effort to reunite with the Catholic Church. Luther, Calvin and Zwingali all believed that there MUST be a reunion with Catholicism or, ONE PROTESTASNT THEOLOGY. Failure to achieve either course, would, in Calvin's words create numerous *contrary* Faiths that will have an **adverse effect on Christianity**.

Even so, had the followers of Luther, Calvin and Zwingali been true to the Teachings of Luther, Calvin and Zwingali, Protestantism might have had a bit of credence. However, the Faiths that these men founded have ALL morphed or fragmented, so that the original Faith of Luther et al, no longer exists.

Luther believed that the *Body* and *Blood* of Jesus were in the Communion Host. Most, if not all Protestant Faiths deny this Catholic Dogma. But this is what Luther taught.

Luther, Calvin and Zwingali all derided Henry for his divorces and labeled Henry a polygamist. Yet today, almost every Protestant Faith allows for Divorce.

Luther, Calvin and Zwingali all taught that spilling the "seed" outside the vagina (Birth Control) was a Sin. Today, the Faiths that are derived from these men advocate Birth Control, a practice that Luther, Calvin and Zwingali, classified as an act against God's plan for creation (Sin).

Now we come to Transubstantiation, a belief that the Body and Blood of Jesus is present in the Eucharist, a belief that was acknowledged by the Founding Fathers of the Reformation, and today, denied by their followers.

Luther had very many Tenets of Faith that coincided with Catholic Theology. None of these Tenets are adhered to by most Protestant Faiths, much less those that "call" themselves Lutherans. What brought about the change in Theology? Which Theologian has declared that Luther was in error, and a teacher of a False Doctrine?

If Luther was in error, then why do you "Lutherans" call yourselves Lutherans? Either you MUST follow his Theology, or you MUST classify him as a teacher of heresy.

YOU CAN NOT HAVE IT BOTH WAYS.

Either Luther is Right and YOU are wrong, or if Luther is wrong then he is a heretic and you are using the name of a heretic for your Faith.

17

SOLA SCRIPTURA
"If it ain't in the Book, You must overlook" *
* A parody on Protestant Theological Beliefs
By
Robert F Kopfer PHD

More times than I can count, I have been told by a Protestant, that if it is not in Scripture, then they cannot accept it. Yet, on the other hand, there are numerous passages in Scripture that are either overlooked or taken out of context, or redefined.

Sola Scriptura is the Corner Stone of Protestantism. It is a Corner Stone that is built on a Foundation of Sand. It is a Foundation that is ever changing and adapting with the "times". Protestantism is like a Ship without a Navigator and a Rudder. As a Ship without a Navigator or Rudder, it is at the mercy of the elements, Elements that are constantly changing.

All Protestant Churches claim to be guided by the *same Bible* and the *same Holy Spirit,* and yet they have come up with as many interpretations of Scripture as there are Churches (Faiths), twenty five thousand or more at last count.

Let me list, just a **FEW** of the differences that have permeated Protestantism:

> Infant or adult Baptism
> Calvinist Predestination or Arminian Free Will
> Once Saved "Always" Saved One can lose Salvation

Is there an assurance of Salvation
Divorce
Abortion
Is Prophecy given?
The Presence of Miracles
Miracles guaranteed if you have faith
Pre-Tribulation Rapture of Christians
Premillenialism or Post millenianism
Validity of Speaking in Tongues
Baptism in the Holy Spirit, Real or deception
Existence of Demons
Body and Blood of Jesus in Holy Communion
Necessity of the Sacraments for Salvation
The Form of Authority within the Church
Are Bishops necessary
Should there be Women Clergy
Homosexual Life style
Icons and pictures of Saints
Drinking Alcohol, Dancing or gambling
Etc, etc, etc

Now here I believe Protestantism has a dilemma All Protestant Faiths ascribe to Sola Scriptura, "The Bible is supreme". According to Protestants of ALL Faiths, Sola Scriptura is the Corner Stone of their Beliefs.

Now, if ALL Protestant Faiths are <u>Guided by the HOLY SPIRIT</u> they should of necessity come up with the same Theology. The Holy Spirit teaches us <u>ONE TRUTH</u>. Therefore there can be only **ONE CHURCH**, not over twenty five thousand separate and distinct Churches, with separate and distinct Teachings.

How can this be the Work of the Holy Spirit?

All Protestants, with whom I have had religious discourse, all proclaim the Doctrine of Sola Scriptura. They reason that if it is not in Scripture, they cannot accept its Teachings. On the other hand, I say to them,

"It is in Scripture and still you do not believe it".

THOU ART PETER AND UPON THIS ROCK I WILL BUILD MY CHURCH

Not only is this paramount in Scripture, but it is then followed by the admonition:

"And the Gates of Hell shall NOT Prevail against It.

Clearly, did not Jesus name Peter as the Head of His Church? Did not Our Lord say that the knowledge Peter had, that Jesus was the Son of God, did not come from man, but from Divine Inspiration?

Knowledge that was a Gift from God.

We have already explained that the Ministry of Peter was in a sense, a duplication of Jesus Ministry. Scripture tells us that Jesus changed Simon's name to Peter (Rock). Scripture tells us that Jesus chose Peter to be present at the momentous periods in His Ministry.

Peter, along with James and John were present at the Transfiguration

Peter walked on water, at Christ's command

Peter, James and John were at Gethsemane

Although John was first to reach the Tomb, he deferred to Peter

Peter was instructed by an Angel, as to Jesus Whishes

Peter cured the lame and the blind, merely by casting his shadow upon the supplicant, just as Jesus did

Peter emulated Jesus, in raising Tabitha from the dead

Peter was "spirited" from prison by an Angel of God

Peter was Crucified

No other Apostle, nor any other man, in the History of Scripture has duplicated the experiences of Peter in emulating the Ministry of Jesus. Surely then, Peter was marked by Our Lord as the Man to Head His Church. Is there not a correlation regarding the presence of Peter, James and John at pivotal moments in Jesus Ministry?

Peter to Lead His Church

James, the first of the Apostles to suffer martyrdom

John had a multitude of responsibilities. The first to look after His Mother, the Blessed Virgin. John wrote the most details of Jesus Ministry, and finally, was the only Apostle to die a natural death, as Jesus had foretold.

There shall be One Fold and One Shepherd

Is this not a passage from Scripture? Is this not the Word from Jesus? Is this not Scripture? Yet my Protestant friends will either deny this passage, or will find a multitude of excuses as to the *"proper"* interpretation.

How can Protestants claim to be of One fold, when there are twenty five thousand different interpretations of the Word of God? Our Lord warned us of "others" coming and preaching in His Name, and that they would be <u>*False Prophets*</u>, and NOT to follow them.

Twenty five thousand different and distinct purported Teachings of the Word of God! This just cannot be.

Sola Scriptura. One Fold, One Shepherd, will the One True Protestant Faith step forward and be recognize, ***if you can!*** *I think not.*

Sola Scriptura. "Unless you are Baptized, etc". Most Protestant Faiths adhere to this admonition, except that many of them will deny infant Baptism. How then can an infant enter the Kingdom of Heaven if it expires before maturity? My Protestant friends will find many excuses for this prohibition against infant Baptism, but they cannot find a passage in

Scripture to bolster their belief. Some Protestant Faiths will even deny Baptism. They say they cannot find a Biblical passage to command Baptism.

One faction (Faith) says it is right, and one faction says it is wrong.

Do we not have a contradiction here?

Sola Scriptura, **"Whose sins you shall forgive, they are Forgiven. Whose Sins you shall retain, they are Retained"** This is clearly not only a Biblical passage, but a Command from Jesus to His Apostles (Church).

It would be ludicrous for one to believe that the Power to Forgive Sins began and ended with Peter and the Apostles. In establishing a Doctrine (Faith), there must be authority. We have but to look at any of the Protestant Faiths and see that in their history, they have morphed and fragmented. NO Protestant Faith today, is the same Faith of their Founders. The Sands of their foundation has shifted and changed its foundation, as the sands upon the beach and the desert shift in response to the winds and the waves.

One Protestant Faith says Yes, and another says No, and another says Maybe. Who is the interpreter of this Biblical passage? Protestants claim they are following the admonition of One Fold one Shepherd. However if this is the case, then the Protestants are speaking in "tongues'.

The Shepherd (Protestantism) speaks, and Flock hears come, and some hear stay, and still others hear go. Is this not confusing to the flock?

One Shepherd has to have ONE Command, not twenty five thousand.

Sola Scriptura. The Protestants, for the very most part do NOT recognize Marriage as a Sacrament, they see no significance in the Biblical passage relating to the Marriage Feast at Cana. I ask you, would Jesus perform His FIRST miracle at the marriage if it was not manifest?

If marriage is only a rite and not a Sacrament, how then would you interpret the passage:

"God Created Man and Woman, and the two shall become One."
"What <u>GOD</u> has Joined Together, let NO man Put Asunder"!

What can more explicit that that admonition by Our Lord as to the Sanctity of Marriage, and yet our Protestant friends will deny the Sacrament of Marriage.

Sola Scriptura, and its interpretations by Protestants, is like going to a buffet. There we pick and chose what we want to partake. So it is with Sola Scriptura and those of the Protestant persuasion, with their interpretation of Scripture.

Now we come to divorce. Does not Sola Scriptura recognize the passage in Scripture that prohibits divorce? How did Jesus answer the Pharisees when they told Him that Moses had given them a "Bill of Divorce"? What was Jesus answer? Was it not:

"Moses gave you a Bill of Divorce, because of your hard heartiness, From the Beginning of Time, God Created Man and Woman, and the Two Shall be ONE.
What God has Joined Together Let No Man Put Asunder!
'For a Man to divorce his wife and Marry another, he shall have committed Adultery. And for another to wed a Divorced person, THEY have committed Adultery."

Some of the explanations given me, regarding the acceptance of divorce by Protestants, are some passage from the Old Testament, or some passage, taken out of context, in the New Testament.

You and I, have witnessed, or know of and read of; countless "couples" who have live in an Adulterous relationship, and yet have had their Union (marriage) "blessed" by a Protestant Minister.

Is this not a contradiction of Scripture (Sola Scriptura)?

What is necessary for someone to become a Protestant Minister? The VAST majority of Protestant Ministers have absolutely no formal Theological education. Many simply declare themselves a "Minister" and form their own Church. They may very well be someone who left Europe or Asia or Africa, because they found better "pickings" here in the States.

Some are "recovering" dope addicts, who are reluctant to divulge the source of their treatment. There are others who are alcoholics, and even pedophiles. There is no source to oversee and or regulate these individuals who "In the name of God" have victimized and led astray millions of Souls who desperately what to "hear the Word of God".

What does it take to become a Protestant Minister, one who can legally officiate at a wedding? One who can visit prisons, and hospitals, and administer social services, and counseling?

All one has to do, is "declare "themselves a Minister. Of Course there is always the "certificate" mill. For only a few dollars, and absolutely no formal theological training, anyone can buy a beautiful, signed, sealed and notarized Certificate of Ordination. A Certificate that allegedly empowers one to declare themselves an Ordained Protestant Minister, who will be recognized anywhere in the WORLD.

To obtain these certificates of Ordination, one need not submit any credentials or submit to a "background "check as their morale character, or to their knowledge regarding theology, These individuals can "preach" any scriptural belief that moves their fancy. Many of these "so called "ministers are filling their pockets with "tithes" that are coerced from their "flock".

For a few dollars, anyone can buy not only a certificate of 'ordination", but also a degree in Divinity (DR) plus a degree in Theology (PHD). No examinations, no Tests, no referrals, No back ground tests, only, at the most, a few dollars. The laxity of the Protestant Movement has, and is, allowing drug addicts, alcoholics, and even pedophiles to become bona fide Protestant Ministers.

There is a "hue and cry" from not only Protestants, but also Catholics, to remove Priests from the ministry, who are accused of violating their vows. <u>This is rightly so</u>. However, I do not hear of any such demands by Protestants to sanction ministers of the Nondenominational Protestant Faiths who are using and abusing their sacred office, to the detriment of women and very minor children.

Sola Scriptura. "Many will come and preach in My Name, do not heed them for they are False Prophets". Did not St Paul warn against dissention? St Paul said that dissention against the Teachings of the Church was WRONG.

<u>Sola Scriptura</u>, there it is in Holy Scripture.

"For a man to lay with a man, as he would a woman, is an abomination (sin)"

Sola Scriptura. Here is another contradiction among those of the Protestant Movement, justification of a homosexual life style. Today, many in the Protestant Movement are advocating the "blessing" of Homosexual unions. There are those Protestant Faiths that have already ordained many individuals who are living in a homosexual relationship. There have been several who have been appointed Bishops, even one who had abandoned his wife and children. There is another minister who "claims" that Jesus was a homosexual. **This is Heresy!** Still another justifies homosexuality be claiming that they were created by God, so we must accept them as such. If we are to accept this premise, them we must accept pedophiles and drunkards as an acceptable life style.

Then again, if we are to ignore the admonition against a homosexual life style, we must then accept incest, for both are called abominations and call for the same punishment. What them of bestiality? Here again, in the same Scriptural passages, these abominations are proscribed. All three Acts are condemned and call for severe punishment.

You cannot accept one, without accepting the others.

All Protestant Faiths *claim* that they are guided by the Holy Spirit. The Holy Spirit, in order <u>to be Omnipotent</u>,

MUST Teach the Truth. There can ONLY be One Truth, not twenty five thousand and more. There can be only one Church Teaching the Word of God.

Our Lord had promised that the "Gates of Hell shall not prevail against It" (Church). Our Lord had also promised that the Advocate (Holy Spirit) would be with the Church until the end of time. Did time stop in the 1500's, I think not.

Can any Protestant Faith show a direct link from Peter to their Faith?

There can be only One Teaching of the Word of God. Therefore if Protestantism is correct, then only one of them is the correct one and the other 24,999 are in error, I firmly believe that ALL 25,000 + are in error.

Many Protestant Faiths teach that Faith Alone is sufficient for Salvation. Other Protestants Faiths will Teach that Good Works alone is sufficient for Salvation. Here we have a contradiction of Sola Scriptura. Protestants preach that for the Word to be accepted, it MUST be in Scripture, but then they advocate a Theology that is NOT in Scripture.

Absolutely, no where in Scripture is there a command or any passage that in the slightest degree suggest that Faith alone is the Key to Salvation. The ONLY two instances of a recording of a Scriptural passage regarding Faith Alone, is by St James where he is explicit in that Faith without Good Works is dead.

Here again we have a divided Protestant theology. One faction says Faith Alone and another says Good Works Alone is sufficient, for Salvation, and yet BOTH factions are wrong. If they are to promulgate the Theology of Sola Scriptura, then they cannot and must not teach something that is not in Scripture. But here they are, teaching Faith Alone, or Good Works Alone, neither has a passage in Scripture.

In the parable of the "Talents", what was the fate of the servant who hid his Talents in the ground? The servant said he had faith in the Master, but he did not utilize his talents for the good of the Master, as the Master expected. Therefore the servant was condemned. As to Good Works, did not Our Lord say that even the Heathens do good to one another, but have no faith in Him?

How can the Protestants claim to be teaching the Word of God, when one faction teaches one way and another teaches another way? They both cannot be right, yet there is no one source within Protestantism to correct the wrongful theology.

In the Parable of the "Sowing of the Seeds", the Apostles asked Our Lord, "Why do you speak in Parable". Our Lord asked them if they knew what he had meant, and Peter replied that they did. Did not Our Lord tell them that it was for them to know and to explain to the people, because (the multitude)

"Seeing they do not see, and hearing they do not hear".

Of all the Christian Faiths <u>only one has taught the same Theology from the Time of Christ, unto today.</u> That Faith is the Catholic Church. Every Protestant Faith that evolved during the time of the Reformation, and others that evolved a few centuries afterward, had changed, morphed, fragmented, divided, combined and evolved into something entirely different than what was originally taught.

Does the Word of God change? Did not Our Lord say:

"Heaven and Earth will Pass Away, but <u>My Word Will Not Pass Away</u>".

Sola Scriptura, One Faith, One Teaching, One Scripture, is what is supposed to be the mantra of Protestantism.

Still we have Protestant Faiths that are teaching a contradictory Scripture, from the Original Teachings of Jesus. Even worse is that the Original "Reformers" were in contradiction with one another, and their followers are in contradiction with their Founders.

From the beginning of the Reformation, there was strong disagreement among the Founders as to what is True Scriptural Theology.

Luther believed that the Body and Blood of Jesus were present in the Eucharist, as does the Catholic Church. Zwingali disagreed.

Bucer taught that the Bible approved of infant Baptism, as does the Catholic Church. Memo Simons disagrees.

Calvin taught that there was NO FREE WILL, and only the "select" were predestined for Salvation or damnation. Others, including the Catholic Church and Melanchthon (Luther's successor) taught that Man had Free Will.

Very many Protestant Faiths do subscribe to the Predestination Theology. If then, only 144 people will be "saved", what is the purpose of Evangelism? If Calvin is right, then the other Churches are Teaching Heresy. Some of the followers of Calvin are the Reform Churches of Holland and the Swiss, including the early Pilgrims. Are not the Baptists and the Congregational Churches, and the Pentecostal and Assembly of God Faiths followers of Calvin and his predestination?

If they are "Right" in their Theology, then all others are teaching heresy. Then again, if they are Wrong, then they are teaching heresy.

A Dutch cleric, Jacobus Arminius rebelled against Predestination, and a modification of Predestination was accepted by some of Calvin's followers. Others, at the Synod of Dort, condemned Arminianism as accepting a Catholic Concept. Here we have another example of dilute and destroy, among the Protestant Faiths.

The Theology of Predestination was adhered to by followers of Calvin well into the 1800's. It was then decided by those Churches that is was better NOT to publicize this Doctrine. Many Reform Churches and other minor Churches did likewise. Baptist, Congregational, Methodist and Presbyterians split into groups of either accepting Calvinism or Arminianism.

Calvinism (Predestination) is against the Teachings of Our Lord. Did not Our Lord tell Peter to go and Teach ALL Nations? If, with Calvin's teachings, only the "elect" are saved, what is the use of Evangelizing. According to Calvin, the Souls are already Elected (selected).

Sola Scriptura. The Bible (Scripture) is the Word of God, and to be adhered too. From the beginning some Churches accepted Calvin's interpretation of Scripture, and some did not. Who then is Right? Then some of followers of Calvin had second thoughts and adopted the Catholic Theology on Salvation.

Calvin depicted God as a vengeful God, selecting a *chosen* few. Catholics believed that God is ALL forgiving, and welcomes the Faithful, those who follow the Teachings of Jesus into His Home (Heaven).

Sola Scriptura. Eternal Salvation. Many Protestants Faiths teach that once you are Saved, you are Eternally Saved. What did Jesus say regarding this? Is it not "Many will fall away..... Many FALSE Prophets will arise and lead you astray, but the ones *who endure* will be Saved".

Jesus, in His Parable of the Sown Seeds tells us of those who had received the Faith, only to lose it when tribulation arises. How is this compatible with *once Saved, always Saved*?

I know many who claim to be Followers of Jesus, *except* that they cannot accept *this Doctrine* or *that Doctrine*, but still say we are followers of Jesus Christ.

Sola Scriptura. Where in Scripture does Our Lord say "Once Saved, always Saved"? Does not Our Lord say that we MUST persevere until the End? "Once Saved, Always Saved" is not a Scriptural Doctrine.

Sola Scriptura. Faith Alone. Here we have another dilemma with Protestantism. Martin Luther preached that one needed *Faith Alone* to attain Salvation. Most Protestants adhere to this Theology. They will quote chapter and verse in Scripture to justify their belief. But what does Scripture "say"? The Parable of the *Talents* and the Parable of *Sowing the Seeds* are quite adamant in stating that Faith Alone is insufficient. There are others passages to *refute Faith Alone*.

St James, the Apostle, tells us about *Faith and Works* in his writings to converts. He admonishes those who believe in Faith Alone, by saying that it is **"no good for a man to have Faith without Deeds"**. Further, St James tells us that **"Faith by itself, if it is not accompanied by action (works) is dead.** St James adds further, "a person is justified by what he does and **NOT by** *Faith Alone*". This is the One and only times the phrase Faith Alone is cited in Scripture, and it tells us that:

Faith Alone is insufficient.

St Mathew tells us, that on the Last Day, God will reward those who Fed Him and Clothe Him and Nursed Him. The Just will reply to Him that they did not know of when they did these good works to Him. Our Lord's reply will be, "that when you did this to the least of my children, you did this to Me.

All believed in Jesus, but only those who did Good Works will be Saved,

Faith Alone is Insufficient.

Martin Luther contradicted himself again by writing that:

"If Good Works do not follow Faith, then Faith in Jesus is Dead".

Protestant Theology is full of contradictions.

Sola Scriptura is paramount, say the Protestants, and yet they distort it, deny it, or ignore it as they see fit.

In an effort to denigrate the Blessed Virgin, Protestants deny the Dogma of the Assumption of the Blessed Virgin (the Mother of Jesus) bodily into Heaven. While the New Testament does not specifically reveal this manifestation, there are passages in the Old Testament to this phenomenon. Passages in the Old Testament tell us of the bodily assumption of Enoch and Elijah plus the probably of Moses also being bodily assumed into heaven.

Here again we have another incidence, in which our Protestant brethren, while claiming Sola Scriptura, ignore Sola Scriptura in an effort to denigrate the Teachings of Catholicism.

Another manifestation that divides Protestantism and Catholicism is the appearance of Saints or Angels to a number of individuals. In denying this manifestation, Protestants are ignoring Scripture.

Sola Scripture, the Protestants say, that if is NOT in Scripture, that they cannot accept it. Scripture is filled with the mention of, not only God, but Angels and Saints interacting with us mere mortals.

Following are but a few of the incidents of Heavenly interaction with mortals:

God and Moses, not once but several times
God and Abraham
Angels and Moses
Angels and Abraham
Angels and Lot
Moses and Elijah with the Apostles
Holy Spirit with the Apostles
Angel with the Blessed Virgin
Angel with Peter
Angel with Joseph
Angels with the Shepherds
Angel with the Magi
Etc,etc,etc

Both the Old and New Testaments are replete with accounts of interaction between mortals and heavenly apparitions. Yet Protestants will deny that any of the manifestations recorded by Catholics ever transpired. This most probably could be that, because there is no record of these manifestations accruing with a Protestant

Here again, we see Protestantism succumbing to the weakening morals of today's society. What I can not understand, is that a Faith that is based on Sola Scriptura, could accept Divorce and Homosexual Acts. Both Acts are prohibited in Scripture. If your Faith is Scripturally based, how can your condoning of these Acts be deemed acceptable?

Sola Scriptura? Dilute and Destroy!

In June 2006, the Episcopalian Faith, in the United States, took steps that will lead to a further fragmentation of "Mainline" Protestant Faiths, in electing as "Lead" Bishop, Katherine

Jefferts Schori. Bishop Schori, if not a homosexual, is at the very least advocating Homosexuality.

Here as I see, is just a bit of confusion. Protestants look to Scripture as a basis of their Faith. "If" it is not in Scripture, then, they cannot accept it as the Word of God. But what does the Head of the Episcopalian Faith here in the United States say, in accepting Homosexual behavior.

In a nationally telecast interview, did not Bishop Schori say that a homosexual "union" was a blessing from God? Did she not say that homosexuals are "special"? How then can Bishop Schori defend this "apparent" contradiction of Scripture, and a contradiction of Sola Scriptura? Protestants cannot have it both ways.

Too Overcome this apparent contradiction regarding homosexuality, Bishop Schori uses (in my understanding) a very lame stupid excuse. Bishop Schori is quoted as using the Old Testament prohibition regarding certain food stuffs and combinations of them. Her reasoning appears to be, that if we can ignore (my word) the prohibitions regarding certain foods and combinations of them, we can then ignore the prohibition regarding homosexuality.

However, to me, it would then be "rational" that if we then accept homosexuality on those premises, we can then accept incest and bestiality, because those acts are classified as an abomination, just as homosexuality. Too accept one, we MUST accept the others.

By ignoring Sola Scriptura in "selected" passages in Scripture, Protestants have tried to justify violations of Scriptural Commands. With the acceptance of homosexuality, divorce, and birth control (spilling of the seed), we can see what has happened to the morals of society Dilute and destroy.

Every founder of the Reformation decried not only homosexual behavior, but divorce and birth control. When did this change in the interpretation of Scripture take place, and by what Theologian?

We have seen where Protestants have given quasi approval

of Divorce, by allowing indiscriminate divorce and remarriage. In so doing they have given tacit approval of adultery.

Further along that line, is *"coveting your neighbor's wife, and coveting your neighbor's goods"*. Let us take Sola Scriptura to its logical conclusion, using Protestant rhetoric, If we are to accept the new Protestant logic, we could then covet *a stranger's wife*, but at the same time, a wife could covet her neighbor's husband, because it is NOT written in Scripture as such.

When Moses descended for Mount Sinai with the 10 Commandments, he found that his people had reverted to Idolatry, and the people of Sodom and Gomorrah also had engaged in a life style of debauchery and homosexuality.

These were deviate behaviors that God had proscribed.

If **Sola Scriptura** is the Cornerstone of Protestantism,

Then **Sola Fide** is the Foundation upon which Protestantism is built

A foundation of Sand.

18

SOLA FIDE

In the very Words of Martin Luther, Sola Fide is the Article upon which the Church (Protestantism) *stands* or *falls.* Sola Fide is by definition "by Faith Alone". Luther used the power of the State (German Nobility) to suppress and persecutes the Anabaptist and others who disagreed with him. It appears that we have a contradiction to Luther's axiom of "any plowman can interpret Scripture". To Believe and interpret belonged *only* to him (Luther), and not to the masses

What is the origin of Sola Fide? It is no where in Scripture. Sola Scriptura? Luther, in *his* interpretation of Scripture into the German language, ADDED the word ALONE to the translation of Romans 3:28

In his writings in 1530, Luther's reply to those who questioned his pronouncement of Sola Fide was,

"It is enough that I have said it. My will is reason enough."

Luther also advised his followers NOT to reply to those who questioned Sola Fide. If a reply must be given, then to say:
"Dr Luther will have it so".

The Cornerstone and Foundation of Protestantism are in my interpretation, Sola Scriptura and Sola Fide. Sola Scriptura the Cornerstone is like limestone, subject to erosion and pitting. We have seen where Sola Scriptura has indeed been morphed, twisted, ignored and misinterpreted.

What then of Sola Fide? Here we have a Foundation of sand, continually shifting. Who can deny that the Theology of Protestantism today, is **vastly** different from the Theology of the Reformation? What Luther, Calvin, Zwingali et al taught, is not accepted as Theology by today's Protestants? When did this metamorphosis take place?

Which Lutheran Theologian, or for that matter, any respected Theologian, was it that declared the Luther was in error? It MUST be that Luther's Theology is in error, as the Lutheran Churches no longer teach the Theology of Martin Luther.

But they still call themselves Lutherans?

I do not understand this concept of naming your Church after someone who's Teachings you do not follow. The same can be said of the Presbyterians, Methodists, Baptists and others.

As far as the "store front" churches, they will teach whatever the "traffic" will allow. That and Anti Catholicism.

Only One Faith is steadfast in its Interpretation of Scripture, from the time of Christ's Ministry, and that is the Catholic Church.

To me, Sola Scriptura and Sola Fide are a contradiction in application. One facet says Scripture is the basis of the Church, while another facet promotes that "Faith Alone" is what is mandatory. Does not one contradict the other?

We have already seen where Sola Scriptura has been used and abused by various Protestant Faiths. Now what of Sola Fide, Faith Alone? By applying the tenet of Sola Scriptura, we see numerous passages that castigate the premise of Faith Alone.

Oh. I'm sorry! I did make a mistake. There IS a passage in Scripture relating to "Faith Alone". It seems that St James (One of Christ's Apostles) has recorded that:

"A man is justified by Works and *NOT by Faith Alone*"
"Faith, by itself, if it has NO Works, is Dead".
"Faith, apart from Works is Dead".

St Paul, a very prolific writer, recorded well over 200 passages relating to "Faith <u>and</u> Works". <u>Never once in ALL his writings</u> did St Paul record that Faith Alone was Scripture. He wrote of the *necessity* of **Faith and Works**, not Faith Alone.

But then, what did Our Lord say regarding Faith Alone? We have already dealt with the Parable of the Talents, whereby the one Servant had "faith" in the Master, but buried his Talents (did not do Good Works) and as a result, the servant was <u>*condemned.*</u>

What then of the rich man, who came to Jesus, and said he "believed" (had Faith) in Him. The rich man then asked to follow Jesus. Did not Our Lord tell the rich man, to give up all he possessed and to give it to the poor (Good Works). The rich man could not do this. So here again, we have Faith without good Works as being unacceptable.

And then, what of the Last Day, when all come before the Lord and proclaim that they had "Faith" in the Lord. Does not Our Lord reply, that they did not "Feed Him or Clothe Him, Visit Him," etc, etc, etc. (Works) and as such, are condemned.

Most Protestants will say that one, who has Faith, will do Good Works. **Hello!** Is this not a contradiction? Does not Sola Fide say "Faith Alone"? If then, Faith is contingent upon Good Works, or Good Works contingent upon Faith, is not Sola Fide an Anathema?

There is a song from my youth that goes:

> "First you say you do,
> Then you say you don't
> Then you say you will
> And then you say you won't
> You got me in the middle
> And won't let me know".

First Luther says Sola Fide, Faith Alone, and then he adds, as do all Protestants, Sola Scriptura, Scriptura Alone. Which is it?

Sola Scriptura contradicts Sola Fide, and Sola Fide contradicts Sola Scriptura.

Luther is recorded as proclaiming that:
The Article upon the Church (Protestantism) Stands or Falls, is
Sola Fide (Faith Alone)

To say that Faith Alone is all that is necessary for Salvation is to deny the Word of Our Lord. How can one believe in the Protestant Tenets, when Protestants cannot believe in them, themselves? There is NO Protestant Faith, since the Reformation, that has not morphed, eroded, fragmented, split, combined and/or was created out of expediency or self aggrandizement.

Among the various Protestant Faiths, there is a VAST difference in what they accept as Scripture. Coupled with that, is that of various Protestant Faiths declaring prohibitions that are not mentioned in Scripture, and yet denying prohibitions that ARE in Scripture.

One has but to look at the ever changing Protestant Theology. The premise appears to be *"what do the people want"*. That then becomes the Theology of the Day. People want divorce; even if it is contrary to Scripture, give it to them. Along with that, let us "close" our eyes to fornication, and even now, accepting homosexual behavior as compatible with Scripture. None of these "adjustments" in Scripture were in the Original Tenets of the Reformation.

Protestantism abhors the Steadfast, never changing Catholic Theology. They claim that the Catholic Church is "out of step" with today's Mores. Moses was faced with this problem, but he would not accept deviating from the precepts of God. Those that were instrumental in fermenting Idolatry were slain.

With Lot, we again have a situation, where the multitude is adverse to the morals prescribed by God. There was no compromise, with this deviate behavior. There was "fire and brimstone".

Some modern day "theologians", are now, not only advocating acceptance of homosexual behavior, but also "blessing" their unions. Sola Scriptura? Absolutely Nowhere in Scripture is there an acceptance of homosexual behavior, and yet, this has become the path of modern Protestantism.

The Founding Fathers of the Reformation, ALL decried fornication, and birth control (spilling of the seed). Yet in a homosexual act, the semen is ejaculated into the anal cavity and mixed with fecal residue. Can any Christian accept this disgusting, filthy and immoral bodily function? Mixing your semen with feces is a perversion of the Gift of God (Sex).

One can Love a homosexual and still abhor the Homosexual sex act.

What has happened, regarding the "eroding" of morality today? Almost all Protestant Faiths give quasi, if not full approval of divorce. Again, this is a complete contradiction of the Tenets of the Founding Fathers of the Reformation. Among Protestants, divorce is the norm, not the exception. Among Christians who follow their Faith and are married in a religious ceremony (Sacrament) the divorce rate is about one or two per 10 marriages, not five or six, as is the case in civil marriages.

What else has happened as a result of the lowering of moral standards? What was once called a "shack up, is now referred as a "significant other". Virginity is now considered abnormal. Home and family were once considered fundamental to a secure marriage. Today it is "how good he/she is in bed. "Try it" before you buy it.

So what is the result?

One third of the babies born today, are to unmarried mothers. A child raised without guidance of both mother and father has a more difficult time emotionally and spiritually. This coupled with the divorced couples who spring a new father/mother every few years on the children. Children have lost the stability of a home and family.

Couples do not work out their problems; they "cut and run". Run in most cases, into the very same problem that they ran away from in the first place.

What else has been the result of the promiscuity that has

been foisted upon society by the *new* moral standards? Twenty five percent of women of child bearing age are inflicted with a sexually transmitted disease. This anomaly is the same for men. Some of the diseases are an inconvenience, but many are incurable.

Many of the sexually transmitted diseases have no cure, some cause sterility and some are fatal. Coupled with this, MILLIONS of babies are aborted each year. We salve our conscience by calling *"it"* a fetus. That fetus is a *human being*. A human being that is on life supports, with every possibility of not only surviving, but most likely will experience a normal healthy and productive life.

I dare you "Pro Choice" advocates that the next time you see a pregnant woman, go up to her and say:

"Congratulations and how is your <u>fetus</u> doing".

The Founding Fathers of the Reformation had looked upon conception as the beginning of life. What is life? Is it not something that is growing? From the moment of conception, the baby (fetus) is a growing Human being.

By aborting the child, you are committing **MURDER.**

In an effort to understand Protestant Theology, I have done much research as to the various Protestant Founders and what has happened to the Faith that they Founded. Plus, I have sent out a survey to hundreds of various Protestant Faiths. The result of my study has very strongly confirmed my Belief and Faith in the Catholic Church.

Before my undertaking, I had accepted Catholicism on Faith, now

I accept Catholicism on Fact.

Our Lord had said to St Thomas:

"You believe because you have seen.
Blessed are they that have not seen, and yet Believe".

There is One Fold and One Shepherd.
A Church Founded by Christ with Peter as the first Pope.

19

SURVEY RESULTS AND COMMENT

In April of 2006, I had sent out several hundred letters containing a survey on Protestant Theology to Mainline, and Nondenominational Protestant Churches plus a number of individuals of the Protestant persuasion. Following is a synopsis of several interesting and surprising responses.

A Nationally known and controversial Methodist Minister was the first to respond. Another Nondenominational Minister sent several emails castigating me for typos, but did not answer the survey. Still another sent several emails, and asking why I did not send the survey via MS Word, and said I did not send enough paper for him to respond. My reply to this Lake Zurich Bible Church Minister was that I would "bring" him all the paper he needed, and that with all the emails he had sent to me, he could have answered the survey with no trouble.

Still another sent an email asking me questions, which I responded, but he "chickened "out from responding.

One respondent denied that she was a Protestant, but that she was a former Catholic. However the Faith that she listed was a Nondenominational Protestant Church. Other individuals, while very vocal, in their Protestant Faith, failed to respond.

Now, we shall see the results of the responses to the survey and my comments.

(1) Denomination of Church
(2) Source of Ordination of Pastor & date

Many, especially nondenominational faiths did not list their denomination, and only one from a nondenominational Church noted how he was ordained. His "ordination" consisted of "laying on of hands" by the church elders. However, their was no information on the credibility of the "elders".

Most of the "pastors" of nondenominational churches did not list the time or source of their "ordination". Very many, I presume, obtained their "ordination" the same way I had. For just a few dollars for a beautiful certificate to a diploma mill, any one can obtain a certificate of ordination. No examination is necessary, only a few dollars. The pastors of a VAST majority of nondenominational faiths have no "formal" theological training. There is no back ground check regarding the morality of these "pastors". Some that I have discovered are "former" drug addicts, former (?) alcoholics, and even former (?) pedophiles. Some are even reluctant to produce evidence of citizenship.

(3) Is your denomination the "One True Teaching of Jesus"
(4) Which denomination is the "One True Church of Jesus"

Several nondenominational faiths "claimed that they were the "One" true Church of Christ. Most others replied that "to believe in Jesus Christ, was the True Faith. However, they all had contradictory Tenets, each teaching a different theology.

(5) Baptism a Sacrament
(24) Should infants be Baptized

As I had foreseen, there is a vast difference in the teachings and beliefs regarding Baptism. Most of the nondenominational faiths look upon baptism as a ritual with no theological significance, while Mainline Faiths do accept Baptism as a Sacrament. Here again we see the diluting of theology, especially by the "Johnny come lately" faiths. Main Line Faiths are themselves divided as to infant Baptism.

Most mainline Faiths look upon Baptism as a Sacrament although several of them do look upon Baptism as a ritual.

Nondenominational faiths deny baptism is a Sacrament All of the respondents quote Scripture as the source of their belief. How can this be?

Some Faiths say yes, some Faiths say No, and still others say it depends. These respondents ALL use the same Bible for their Theology, and yet they have all come up with vastly different interpretations. Where is the Holy Spirit that they claim guides them?

(6) Was Calvin Justified in the sentence he imposed on Cervetus

The answers and lack of acknowledgement of this question intrigued me. One respondent corrected my deliberate typo (Cervantes) regarding Cervetus name. This individual emailed me several times regarding this item and others, but then failed to respond to the survey. He was just one of several, who would spend a great deal of time corresponding with me about the survey, and then decline to put their Belief in writing.

Only one respondent stated that the punishment was too severe. ALL others, either left the answer blank, or admitted that they have no knowledge of the incident.

(7) Which Lutheran Denomination follows the original Theology of Martin Luther

No Lutheran denomination responded to this survey, for if they had, they would have to admit (in writing) that they do not follow the Theology of their Founder. At the same time, Lutheran laity has admitted that they do not know the answer.

Most nondenominational Faiths replied that either they did not know, or did not care, as it was of no concern to them.

NO concern regarding the Theology that led to the Reformation? How can this be? This clearly shows that a VAST majority of the nondenominational ministers are lacking in Theological and Biblical knowledge.

(8) Is sex outside of marriage, fornication

Only one respondent approved of sex out side of marriage. He justified the sexual act, by reasoning that "if" two people love one another it is proper and is with God's blessing. He is of the Methodist persuasion. No other denomination, Mainline or Nondenominational approved of unmarried sex. ALL classified the act of fornication, as is proscribed in Scripture.

We have but to look at the statistics relating to unwed mothers and abortions to see that quasi approval of sex outside of marriage is an abomination.

(9) Is Timothy St Paul's Brother
(14) Is Phillip Peter's brother

I received a various answers to these questions, but for the most part, the answer was that he was not a "blood" brother. Some did not reply to this question, and others said they were "spiritual" brothers. One went so far as to imply that I should know better, that Timothy and Paul could NOT be brothers as one was a Jew and the other a Gentile. The respondent failed to note that Timothy's mother was a Jewess, which in Jewish Law made Timothy a Jew.

Another "mainline" minister replied facetiously, "who cares" whether they were brothers. This is hardly an intelligent reply to a theological question. There are many references to "brother and sister" in scripture, and the reason in bringing forth these two questions at this time is that they are intertwined with question (18), as we shall explore later.

Both St Peter and St Paul referred to Phillip and Timothy as "brothers", when in matter of fact; they were related only in *Spirit,* not blood.

(10) Do you believe that Jesus was born of a Virgin
(18) Do you believe that Jesus had siblings thru Mary

Now here we have a real dilemma. Most Faiths replied that indeed, Jesus was born of a Virgin as prophesied in Scripture. Yet, a Minister of the Methodist Faith said NO. He explained that God did NOT work *supernaturally*

Too deny that God works supernaturally, is to deny the parting of the Red Sea, the Resurrection, the Ascension, walking on water, feeding 5000 with 5 loaves and two fishes, raising of the dead, etc, etc, etc. Too deny that God works supernaturally, is to not only deny the Divinity of Jesus Christ, but to cast aspersions upon His Ministry, Passion, and Resurrection and Ascension bodily into Heaven. Without these precepts, there is no Christianity, and this is tantamount to saying that Jesus is not God.

This is Heresy! This a faction of Protestantism, that is ignored by those that preach Sola Scriptura as The Word of God, and embrace this denomination as Brethren in Christ!

As to #18, and the alluded siblings of Jesus, I have found that EVERY one of the Founders of the Reformation were firmly in the Belief that Mary was a Perpetual Virgin. As a Perpetual Virgin, she had abstained from carnal relations ALL her life.

Martin Luther has stated that to deny the Perpetual Virginity of Mary, is to deny the Divinity of Christ. Not only was this the Theology of Luther, but also ALL the major Theologians at the time of the Reformation.

Each and every one of the Theologian at the Reformation had explained that the word for "brother and sister" in Scripture, referred to cousins and clan members. This theology is not only Catholic, but also ALL of the original founders of the Reformation. All of them taught that to deny the Perpetual Virginity of Mary would denigrate the Divinity of Jesus and would be considered heresy.

So who are the heretics? Is it Luther, Calvin, Zwingali, Wesley, et al, or is it the modernist who has hijacked Protestantism?

Dilute and destroy the credo of those who subvert the Word of God.

The Catholic Faith has not diluted or changed its Theology for well over 2,000 years, yet the Protestant movement has in many instances reversed its theology over 180 Degrees since the 1520's.. What was taught by the Protestant movement then as Scripture, is today, heresy.

Who are the Theologians that condemn Luther, Calvin, Zwingali, et al?

(11) Was Calvin correct in his prediction to Melanchthon

Most respondents left this questioned unanswered. Several did reply that they were unfamiliar with this incident in theological history. Some had said "this was not covered" in their studies.

It seems obvious to me, that the reason All Protestant ministers and laity are unfamiliar with Calvin's warning regarding Protestantism, is that Calvin was correct in predicting the diluting of the Reformation by many "False" prophets of which they are one.

All Protestant Faiths proclaim that they are teaching the Word of God, and yet, each and every one of them has a contradictory Theology.

Dilute and destroy. This is exactly what Calvin predicted.

(12) Is Communion a Sacrament

Here again we have contradictions. Many mainline Faiths replied that Holy Communion is a Sacrament, ordained by Jesus Christ, while most nondenominational Faiths along with the Baptist replied that it is a ritual.

Here again we are beset by contradictions in Theology. All of these Faiths use the same source for Scripture, and each and every one has derived at a diverse answer.

Chip, chip, chip away at the cornerstone of Protestantism. Dilute and destroy.

(13) Is Tradition a basis for Scripture
(36) When were the FOUR GOSPELS declared HOLY SCRIPTURE
And by what source

All Protestants replied NO to question #13, and had puzzling answers for #36. The two, while I separated them on purpose, are intrinsically related. One is dependant upon the other.

First let us look at the response to the question regarding the Four Gospels. Only ONE respondent cited the acceptance of the four Gospels as Holy Scripture, in the 4th century by the Church Council (Catholic) after due deliberation, and prayer. This respondent is a "lapsed" Catholic.

Most Protestant Ministers replied that it was in the *first century*.

Hello there Do you not understand the question?

The question was, "**when** were the four Gospels *declared* Holy Scripture, not when were they written. We all know, that they were written shortly after the resurrection and ascension of Jesus, which would indicate that they were written within the first century.

However, there were many WRITINGS regarding Jesus and His Ministry. It was the **Catholic Church** Council, three hundred years **after** the ascension of Jesus that after study and prayer, ordained that the Gospels of Mark, Mathew, Luke and John, along with various letters from St Paul and others, were in deed and fact, Holy Scripture.

How then was the Church governed during those three hundred plus years? Was it not by TRADITION? Until about 387 A D, there was no "Holy Scripture". Scripture itself is replete with the admonitions in both Old and New Testaments, to adhere to;

Tradition.
Tradition preceded Holy Scripture.

Both St Peter and St Paul called upon the faithful to uphold *traditions.*

(15) Is sex between men an acceptable Christian behavior
(22) Should your Denomination bless a marriage between homosexuals
(37) Should a marriage between brother and sister be acceptable

(41) Should a marriage between Uncle/Niece or Aunt/Nephew
Be acceptable

Only one minister replied that Homosexual behavior was compatible with a Christian Life Style. The irony here is that his denomination is, on record, of opposing the homosexual act, at the present time. It is, like ALL Protestant Theology, subject to change.

All Nondenominational Faiths abhor homosexuality, and incest.

What I found interesting with the Methodist minister who believes in homosexual unions, gave a some what evasive answer to # 37. While he did reply that is was not acceptable, he did qualify his answer by saying it was unacceptable *due to genetics*. Modern science has deflated this myth, by noting that the incidence of genetic abnormalities is just about 2% higher when compared with a normal sexual union. He did not reject the union of brother and sister for Scriptural reasons.

(16) Do you believe in Purgatory
(35) Is Purgatory exclusively a Catholic Belief

Here ALL Protestant Faith are united. However they do not look at not only Scripture, but very early Christian beliefs. By early, we mean in the first several hundred years of Christianity. Writings in the catacombs are replete with request for the faithful *to pray for a departed Soul*.

What use is there to pray for the departed? If they are in Heaven, they need no prayers, and if they are in Hell, no amount of prayer will aid them. Therefore logic tells us, that we are praying for the dead, who are in Limbo (purgatory), to aid in cleansing their Souls. Hebrew scripture refers to a purgatory like entity.

(17) Is the Rite of Marriage a Sacrament

Every Protestant respondent referred to Marriage as a "ritual", not a Sacrament. Jesus preformed His first miracle at the "Wedding Feast at Cana". Is it not logical that by 'honoring" the wedding with a miracle, that the wedding has special significance.

Then what of the admonition by Jesus regarding divorce? Marriage is mandated by God for the purpose of procreation. Sex outside of marriage is fornication. If marriage is but a ritual, then it would negate the "bonds of matrimony" and give quasi approval to fornication, all of which we know, is condemned in Scripture.

At every Protestant marriage ceremony that I have attended, there is not one where the Minister does NOT proclaim;

"We are Gathered here in the Sight of God".
"To Unite this Couple in Holy Matrimony"

If God is present and the "service" is for purposes of a Holy Union, it is not logical that it MUST be a Sacrament.

(19) Is dancing a Sin
(22) Is partaking of alcohol a Sin
(31) Is the game of "chance" a Sin

All those who responded gave a qualified approval to dancing and drinking.

With regard to #31, only one minister qualified "gambling" as a Sin as "we" would be using God's money for ill gotten gains, or wasting the money.

However, you and I know that there are several Faiths that forbid not only alcohol, gambling and dancing but also consumption of caffeine.

(20) Has any member of you denomination past or present
Experienced the Stigmata

Not one single Protestant Faith replies with an affirmative. None of their congregation had been so "blessed". I have been able to discover over 230 instances of the Stigmata, from the time of St Francis of Assisi unto today. Every one has been of the Catholic Faith. I was unable to find any of the Protestant Faith so Blessed.

Some physiatrists have "reasoned" that the phenomenon is perhaps caused by hysteria. How ludicrous it is for them to imply that only Catholics are fanatic in their religious beliefs.

Padre Pio and Therese Neumann were subjected to independent examinations, by Protestant doctors and nurses, and all were convinced that the Stigmata's are a true physical experience. Many of the medical personnel later did convert to Catholicism.

There is a mentally challenged young girl, in New England, who is undergoing the Stigmata. Here again, she is of the Catholic Faith, and here again, several of her Protestant nurses have converted to the Catholic Church.

We are not talking about several hundred years ago, we are relating to experiences that have happened and ARE happening in my life time.

> (22) Has any member of your Denomination been "visited
>   "by Saints
>
> or Angels
>
> (30) Do you Pray to a Saint or Angel to intercede for you

Here again, we have no Protest response in the affirmative. It must be because the Protestants do not recognize honoring Saints.

Catholics do pray to Saints, but the prayer is for the Saint to intercede for them, with God. There are many recorded events, in Catholic history, of Saints visiting the faithful. Many of these occasions are replete **with physical evidence** of a Miracle.

As Joseph and the Magi were visited in a dream by Angels of the Lord, so was I. It was an experience that set me on my path to full acceptance of Catholicism.

My wife, not only was physicallysaved by two Angels, but also had the "blessing" to experience the departing of the Soul of Nun at the moment of her death.

She held the hand of Sister Louise, the head Nun at the Home, at the very moment of her death. She swears before God, that she saw a white vapor leave the body at the moment of her death.

As the Nuns knelt, crying for their beloved leader, Shirley turned to them and asked, "Why are you weeping? Today she is in Paradise with our Savior".

Not only have I experienced Miracles as a result of Praying to a Saint, for intersession, but we have witnessed the results of prayer in several parts of the world. In visiting several Churches and Shrines, we have seen thousands of crutches of those who were cured festooning the pillars of churches and thousand of letters relating to the experience of a miracle.

Is it fantasy or reality? If it is fantasy, why is it only Catholics experience these events? Are only Catholics fanatics? I think not.

Here again, Scripture is replete with accounts of "Saints" and Angels in communication with us mortals.

Very many Catholics and a goodly number of Protestants have been seen displaying a medal of St Christopher. This is a "request" (prayer) beseeching a safe journey. Many a parent has prayed to their child's Guardian angel, to protect their loved ones from physical and Spiritual harm.

I know personally, that my Guardian Angel has several times, saved me from not only physical harm, but also Spiritual Harm.

(25) Should the Ordination of a Minister be a Sacrament

All respondents were adverse to the ordination of a minister being a Sacrament. Many professions require schooling and an examination followed by a license to function in their profession.

With *most* Protestant ministers, there is no examination required. There are some who will attend Theological Seminary. What I find interesting is that five individual will attend the same Seminary and go to five different Denominations, each of which, will have a contrary Theological regimen.

Here I find an enigma. Protestants, like all parents, will demand that the teachers in our schools have proper certification as to competence and their knowledge of the subject that they would be teaching. These very same Protestant parents will allow their children, and themselves to be "taught" the most Holy Scripture by individuals who have absolutely no Theological certification.

These "ministers" of God, would have no formal theological education. There would have been no referrals as to character and morality.

Some of my family, and friends had invited me to come and listen to the Sermon given by their Pastors. I did contact these individuals, and they did invite me to "listen to them preach".

My reply was that I have heard and witnessed "great" orators, Hitler, Tammy Faye and Jim, plus David Koresh and others. Each led their flock to destruction. What I wanted was to talk to them face to face, and ask them questions regarding their Theology, and have them explain it to me, and allow me to question them.

All of them were too busy to meet with me.

In Protestantism, there is no One Theology, there are many deviate faiths. How does this equate with the Mandate;

"One Fold, One Shepherd."

(26) Do you believe that St Peter was in Rome.

Here again, I was amazed by the responses. One was facetious and wrote "who cares". Most others said it did not matter, or they had no idea. This is a far cry for only several years ago, when many Protestant Evangelists, in denouncing the Catholic Faith, claimed that St Peter was *never* in Rome.

Here again, the Protestant detractors were refuted. There are letters written by St Peter while he was in Rome, but there are also historical accounts of St Peter Baptizing converts in the Tiber River.

Then there is the archeological find in the 1960's under the Vatican, just where "tradition" indicated the remains of St Peter would be.

Some of my early proponents derided the Papacy starting with Peter. They would claim how can he be the first Pope if he were never in Rome. This is tantamount to saying that George Washington was not our first President, because he was never in Washington D C. It is ludicrous to say the very least.

(27) What is your source of Authority for **interpretation** of Scripture
(49) Was Luther correct in his Belief that "any Plowman can interpret
The Bible"

The response to these two questions utterly amazed me. First off, there was a universal response naming the King James Bible. Alto one nondenominational minister did cite the *Saint James Bible*. It was most probably, a typo?

What had been asked, in the survey, was "what is the **SOURCE** of interpretation. We here in the USA know that the *Constitution* is our Political Bible. However we also KNOW that the *interpretation* of the Constitution is exclusively the purview of the Supreme Court.

All responses to #49 were in the affirmative. All believed that Luther was correct, in stating that *"anyone"* can interpret Scripture. We can see the fallacy of this pronouncement, by viewing the plethora of contradictory Beliefs, by any and ALL Protestant denomination.

We may interpret a legal document as we would like it to be, but in reality, it is the Court that has the "final decision". Protestants interpret Scripture as they would like it to be.

To listen to a dozen Protestants, of various denominations, espousing their Beliefs, one would appear to be at the *Tower of Babel*. Each and everyone are citing and quoting vast contradictory interpretations of Scripture. Only one facet do they have in commonalty, **Anti Catholicism**.

Luther's pronouncement is in fact, **hypocrisy.**

Catholics interpreted the Scriptures, Luther said they were WRONG.

The Anabaptists interpreted Scripture, and Luther said they were WRONG.

How can this be, if ANYONE can interpret Scripture? If Luther is correct, then there are twenty five thousand different interpretations of the Word of God!

How does this equate with **"One Fold and One Shepherd"**?

It is truly written;

"They have eyes to see and do not see, and ears to hear and do not hear".

(32) Is Oral or Anal sex a Sin

Here again we have received contrary pronouncements. The Ministers, who advocate and promote Homosexuality, believe that it is a "loving" expression, and God is Love.

Most Protestant ministers and laity were revolted by these abnormal sexual acts, and classified them as a Sin against God. What puzzles me is, they will protest the "spilling" of the Seed, into the Anal or Oral cavity, but have no objection to spilling the same Seed into a condom.

One of the laity gave a qualified assent to this Act. She believed it was proper when consummated between husband and wife.

Here we have the followers of Luther, Calvin, Zwingali, et al, condoning a practice that these Founders of the Reformation classified as an abomination and an Act against the Laws of God.

(33) Is Abortion an acceptable Christian practice
(34) At what point does life begin

All Protestant respondents replied that abortion was contrary to God's Law. There was one exception to this belief, by some of the respondents, that being IF the life of the mother was threatened.

IF Protestants were united in Fact instead of "belief" there would not be a million abortions a year. As far as I am concerned, Protestants give lip service regarding abortions.

Most of the respondents believed that life began a conception, a **Catholic Dogma**. Some believed it began within a few weeks.

Catholic doctors, nurses and other medical staff have fought the "legal" system to gain the "right" to not participate in these acts of killing babies. I know of NO PROTESTANT denomination that has taken any Court action to protect their members, or has warned their members, that the "killing" of babies (abortion) is a grievous Sin.

(38) Is prostitution a Sin
(40) Should a man be allowed several wives

All respondents replied in the affirmative. Most, as ALL "good" Protestants do, quoted chapter and verse, decrying the acts of prostitution.

With polygamy, most respondents just said that it was wrong, *because of State laws*. Here we are talking about God's Law, and they do not quote Scripture, but State and Federal Laws.

Are we then to believe, that IF the State or Federal Government approves a Law, contrary to Scripture, then Religion MUST accept these Laws?

We have already seen, where Martin Luther, unlike the Catholic Pope, who refused Henry a divorce, gave, as a matter of expediency, approved of Bigamy (Polygamy) to a German Nobel, in return for aid and protection.

(39) Does a Minister have the Authority to "forgive" Sins

Here we have unanimity among the respondents. Not a single Protestant minister or even members of the laity noted the Scriptural Passage where Jesus said to His Apostles (Church);

"Whose Sins You Shall Forgive, they are Forgiven".

Do you honestly believe that Jesus gave this Power to the Apostles, and only *them*, for that particular generation? Do you honestly believe that Jesus established a Faith, (Church), and would vest NO Authority within it.

That would be like building a Theology on a Foundation of Sand.

(42) Do you believe there is a Hell
(43) Do you believe in Predestination

Most respondents believe that there is a Hell. However, there were those that said, NO. They explained that God is ALL Loving and would forgive us, and on the Last Day, would Welcome us into His Home.

What a "crock" of drivel. These were the very Ministers who profess the Authority of Scripture (Sola Scriptura). Scripture is replete with passages wherein Our Lord warns of disobeying God's Law, and what the punishment would be.

"They shall be cast into Hell's Fire, where there shall be weeping and wailing and gnashing of teeth".

If there is NO Hell, and Our Lord will forgive ALL our transgressions, on the Last Day, why then is there a necessity to follow God's Law, since, as spoiled children, we will ALL be forgiven anyway.

Some of the respondents believe in Predestination, and some do not. Here again we have the same enigma. If it is already determined who will be "Saved" and who will rot in Hell, why then Evangelize? Why "try" to live by God's Laws, since it already has been determined, that no matter how good or how bad we are, we can do nothing to change our destination (Salvation).

(44) Do you believe that "Faith" Alone will secure Salvation
(45) Do you believe that "Acts" Alone will secure Salvation

Here again, we have a contradiction in Protestant Theology. Here are two contrary Theological Beliefs, espoused by various Protestant Faiths. One Faith says Right, another says Left, then One says Go, and another says Stay. Which is it?

Protestants do not hesitate to point out the "alleged" wrongs within the Catholic Church, but are mute, regarding Heresies' with the Protestant Community.

If "Faith Alone" is Scripture, then "Acts Alone" is a violation of Scripture. If then "Acts" Alone are Scripture, then "Faith Alone" is a violation of Scripture.

Most Protestants are so wrapped up in their own theology, that they cannot see the Heresies around them. They ONLY concentrate on their Anti Catholic rhetoric.

(46) Do you believe that Islam is a threat to Christianity
47) Do you believe that Islam and Christianity can coexist
(48) Do you believe that Luther was correct in his praise of Suleiman

Here we unanimity among the Protestants, regarding Islam being a threat to Christianity.

Christianity teaches that if you do not embrace the Christian Faith, you will suffer in the "Life hereafter"

Islam teaches, convert or die (NOW). Islam teaches that it is proper to kill Christians and Jews, or any who do not embrace Islam.

There were several ministers who believed that Islam and Christianity can coexist. These were the ministers who approved of homosexuality. What a paradox! To think *you* can coexist with a Faith that condemns the very obnoxious, immoral and unnatural act that *you* promote.

There is no doubt that should Islam become the Law of the Land, those whose life style that you espouse, would be among the first to feel the wrath of Islam (death).

As to Luther and his praise of Suleiman, All of the respondents wrote that either they were unfamiliar with this "incident" and could give no opinion.

(50) Are the Lutheran and Anglican Faiths wrong in continuing dialogue

Regarding reunification

Most Mainline Protestant thought any dialogue was good. However some Nondenominational Faiths said they did not care. Even were the Faiths to reunite, THEY would NOT.

Where is the Belief;

One Fold, One Shepherd

This is a precept that Protestantism does not espouse.

Epilogue

As a youth I was "born" into the Catholic Faith. Between my parents and the good Nuns, the Order of St Francis, at St Williams School in Chicago, I learned about my Catholic Faith. At that time, I accepted the Teachings of the Catholic Church, on Faith.

After three years of studying the various Protestants Faiths and their Founders, I was given a "Certificate" of Ordination by the "**Jesus of Nazareth Church International (JONCI)**. There was no examination, or any test of any kind. There was no background check to see if I was a pedophile, or drug addict, or even if I had ANY knowledge of Scripture, and yet they awarded me a Doctorate in Religion, plus a PHD in Theology.

With these (bogus) credentials I could, if I so desired, establish a Protestant Church (Faith). I could, If I so desired, teach my own brand of Scripture, officiate at marriages, give counseling, visit hospitals and prisons, which IS happening in establishment of thousands of bogus Protestant Churches.

Not only did JONCI award me these "honors", but also, for a paltry $25.00 awarded me the rank of Bishop.

JONCI is not the only "diploma" mill, in my opinion. The internet is replete with scores of web sites to accord the ways and means to become a Protestant Minister.

No examinations, no background checks, no theological knowledge, no proof of citizenship just a few "bucks and you are a fully *accredited* Protestant minister. So we can readily see why there are over twenty five thousand different Protestant faiths, all of them teaching their own brand of "Christianity".

Give the people what they want, is the theology of the Day. This flies in the face of the command of Jesus;

There Shall Be One Fold, and One Shepherd.

One of the lessons I learned, is that "A prophet is without honor in his Home".

What I had accepted, on **Faith,** as a youth, I today, as an adult, accept as **Fact.**

The Catholic Church has the One True Teaching of Jesus Christ.